SECRETS

Unlocking the Mysteries of
Successful Advertising

Jeff Resnick

Writers Club Press
San Jose New York Lincoln Shanghai

Secrets
Unlocking the Mysteries of Successful Advertising

Writers Club Press
an imprint of iUniverse.com, Inc.

For information address:
iUniverse.com, Inc.
5220 S 16th, Ste. 200
Lincoln, NE 68512
www.iuniverse.com

ISBN: 0-595-19375-7

Printed in the United States of America

Thanks to the beautiful women in my life:
Cass, Jennifer, Jessica, and, of course, Emma Jane.

CONTENTS

INTRODUCTION

I've spewed more Advertising copy than you can shake a stick at! After writing no less than 10,000 commercial scripts, and producing the equal number of finished Radio and TV spots for broadcast in hundreds of cities across North America, I couldn't help but become accomplished at my tasks. So much so that my clients marveled at my perceived ability to conceptualize, write, *and* produce a 60-second commercial...in but 30-seconds. And that's what I enjoy most about writing commercials. You have no choice but to make your point, quickly. Get in, get out, no extraneous words allowed. Eventually, your mind adjusts to thinking in 60-second blocks of time, much like the internal clock that wakes you at the appropriate hour each morning despite your desire to sleep in. But this is the first book I've written. Initially, I found it impossible to take more than a minute to write each chapter, until I became accustomed to a book being a "long form" project, whereas a commercial is a "short form" project. So, I practiced this new craft with diligence, discarding my stopwatch along the way. I learned to regard the book as nothing more than a compilation of chapters, each chapter merely a collection of 60-second paragraphs composed of sentences, groups of words which are, after all, only harmless alphabet characters! By approaching the book in this way, it started to fall together, despite my journalistic inexperience.

I learned another important lesson. Like a doctor in the midst of flu season, who knows and expects that 99% of sick patients on any given day will complain of fever and aching muscles, my patients' symptoms were always complaints of too few customers or too few dollars to attract them. I came to rely on my own bedside manner of trusting my first instinct. Frankly, I had no choice. When you're working in the retail environment, there simply isn't time to think! That's why I always avoided clients who thought they needed constant rewrites. They found out, as I did, that we invariably ended up right where I had started, but by that point too tired of the process to be interested in completing it. On the other hand, writing a book has proven to be quite the opposite. I find I'm constantly rewriting chapter after chapter, having slept on an idea for weeks at a time. As a novice, I naturally assumed that the best place to start writing a book would be the **Introduction**, since it should establish the very premise for the writing. I couldn't have been more wrong! I'm reworking this introductory chapter today, long after having finished writing the book, because I've experienced some important and meaningful revelations that weren't part of my thought process when I started the project. Plus, something else happened that has compelled me to take this book to publication. After a 25-year absence from the college classroom, where I enjoyed a 6-year stint as a Professor of Music in the 1970's, I'm returning to my educational roots as Visiting Professor of Advertising and Marketing at a large state university. When I began examining the texts I'd be using, I immediately realized that not even one of them focused on what I consider to be the essential elements of Advertising! Don't get me wrong, there are some wonderful text books out there, written by some very diligent and talented people. But strip away all the hoopla about national trends, statistical analysis, market research, focus groups, and the like, and you're left with remarkably little information or discussion about the driving force behind the "real world" of Advertising. The focus seems to be "How to Succeed on Madison Avenue." That's fine for the few students who will choose that path, or be chosen by it. But what about the other 99% of students who will undoubtedly spend their careers on Main Street America, working to address the challenges faced by the hundreds of thousands of business owners who don't even know where Madison Avenue is…and don't care? Unfortunately, so much of the material presented in the college classroom proves irrelevant to the realities these students (and their clients) will face in the trenches. We shouldn't be surprised. That's the way it is in any field of study.

Advertising is so much more than Art or Science. It's all about People, and how they interact. Merchants, customers, and vendors all interact, as People, in ways that will ultimately determine not only the nature of Advertising, but the very success or failure of any business. When all is said and done, Advertising should reflect not only what your business is all about, but also who you are, as a person. Once you come to grips with this basic premise, you'll begin to realize that consumers will respond to you not only as a business owner with products or services to sell, but as a person behind the curtain of your Advertising program. "Pay no attention to that man behind the curtain!" Even the Wizard of Oz found out there's no curtain large enough to conceal your intentions. Likewise, you, as a person, will determine the nature of the interaction with your Advertising vendors, including account executives from ad agencies, TV and Radio stations, newspapers and magazines, graphic artists, media producers and directors, and a whole myriad of people you've yet to meet. When I began writing, I knew I wanted to share some of my personal Advertising experiences with you, but I wasn't sure how to do that. Once I allowed my fingers to do the walking on my computer keyboard without a conscious thought of the direction the words might take, the chapters more or less *belched* themselves out! It was then that I realized I wasn't writing about Advertising as much as I was writing about People. I've met and worked with some wonderful People over the span of my Advertising career, and now that I'm writing about those experiences, I have come to understand that the Advertising is always shaped by the People, sometimes subtly, sometimes not. As you might expect, I've also worked with some not-so-wonderful People, and I've learned that the resulting Advertising always suffers. If nothing else, I hope you'll be able to step back and view yourself the ways others will view you. The best advice I can offer you is to be yourself in everything you do, from developing your Advertising program to interacting with the many People you'll come in contact with along the way. I sincerely believe that if you remain true to yourself, to your underlying values and principles, you can't help but be more successful both in your personal relationships and your business relationships. In fact, having said that, I'm reminded that it was always the not-so-wonderful People who attempted to convince me that one must separate personal values from business values, since those two value systems must be in conflict before financial success can be achieved. I never fell into that trap. And I never will.

Advertising has been called a vicious, competitive, cut throat industry. Should you expect anything less for the very life-blood of your business? On the premise that the purpose of Advertising is to motivate potential consumers to shop (and buy) at your business rather than someone else's, then Advertising should be of prime concern to the financial health of your business. Unfortunately, it is often the most misunderstood and ignored business building block, relegated to the back-room pile of "I'll think about it when I have time" projects. You never will, because you'll never have the time. When it's too late, you'll see the need to hire an "expert" to figure it all out for you. The problem is, experts are few and far between, and you can't afford to hire one anyway, because experts don't work cheap! (If they did, who would believe they were experts?) Maybe you'll take a course at the local community college (when you have the time) and become your own expert. Except the college probably doesn't offer a course on Advertising. And if it does, the instructor will be younger than you are, and won't have a clue, either, which explains why he's teaching the class instead of operating his own successful business. OK, you'll go to the library and do some research (when you have the time), only to find shelves of books about how to prepare a business plan, how to get a business license, how to hire a lawyer, and how to hire a lawyer to sue your lawyer. These books will fall into one of two categories. One, the book will be so general as to be irrelevant. If you're lucky, it might have a chapter on Advertising, the sum and substance being that you really should Advertise. Gee, thanks. Second, the book will be so overburdened with useless statistics and number crunching that it'll be of little use or interest to anyone except a Ph.D. in Advertising. (Is there such an animal?) Sooner or later, you'll come to the unpleasant realization that you're knee deep in kaka.

I can all too clearly remember my college orientation as an incoming freshman in 1965. (Has it really been that long?) The dean confronted our group of 2,500 by warning, "Look to your left, now look to your right. The person you're looking at on either side of you won't make it through freshman year!" Similarly, you've surely heard the statistic that 85% of all new businesses fail within the first year. But not yours. No, you planned your business with an idea that you were convinced could work, with the dream of being your own boss, with a vision of making your own decisions about your future, with the belief in your innate ability to succeed where others may have failed. As you contemplated your future business empire, it's totally understandable that Advertising received the level of attention inverse to its importance. Rightly so, Advertising was the least of your worries. You were too busy trying to convince a banker that you knew what you were talking about when you weren't totally convinced in your own mind that you really did. You were too busy trying to find that "location, location, location" that all the real estate agents told you would make or break your business. You were too busy trying to figure out where you would find employees who would do everything you told them to do, as soon as you told them to do it, the way you yourself would do it, and all for minimum wage or less. Yes, you were too busy with all the "little things" that you have to do before you can open the front door and invite your customers in. Customers? You never really thought about where those customers would come from, how they would know about you and your dream, or whether they would even care once they did know. You just assumed they would. Like I said, that's totally understandable.

If you're already in business, think about how you felt that first morning as you opened your doors. Then think about how you felt at the end of that first day, first week, first month, and first year, if you were one of the 15% lucky enough to make it that far. If you're not yet a business owner, but contemplating becoming one, think about how it might feel to throw a party where nobody shows up. Think about it now, not later, because the ultimate success of your party is determined the moment you make the decision to throw the party, well before the party itself ever starts. How could you know your intended guests would never receive your invitation? How could you know they might receive it but neglect to read it? How could you know your invitation could arrive the day *after* the party? How could you know your invited guests might have other plans that were more important to them than your party was to you? Operating a business is much like throwing a party…every day. It costs money, and it takes a ton of planning and hard work. But when your guests finally depart with a smile and tell you they had a wonderful time, you invariably leave the cleanup until morning and collapse into bed knowing that you just threw one heck-of-a party. And, despite your fatigue, you can't sleep because you're already thinking about your next party! Are you nuts, or what?

This book is really about throwing a successful party at your place of business, every day. I'll be sharing 20+ years of experience with you, giving you advice that will be relevant to some of the harsh realities you'll be facing, citing real examples of real people in real business situations. Think of me as the expert you'd like to hire, but can't afford to. I conclude this **Introduction** by assuring you this book is *not* about Madison Avenue, and it's not at all about the business world's self-proclaimed big boys. While I had the pleasure of working with many large businesses, I was always more comfortable in the trenches with small business owners. In fact, I found out that many large businesses are often nothing more than a group of small businesses banding together for the perceived common advantage. Theoretically, the whole must be greater than the sum of the parts, though it rarely proves true! If you really must know, most of the big boys I came in contact with were, to my way of thinking, quite small, if you catch my drift. I hope you'll read on. If you do, you'll meet some very nice People who have experienced many of the challenges you'll face in unlocking the closely-held **secrets** of successful Advertising.

WHO AM I TO TELL YOU, ANYWAY?

I have a sign on my door that reads, "Expert." Even better, I have a web site, and my own domain name! As you probably know by now, an expert is anyone who says he's one, especially in the wacky world of Advertising. The web site is just icing on the cake. And that's the problem. At the end of the day, who am I to tell you anything, anyway? Isn't it my obligation to explain how I became an expert, so you can decide if reading this book will be worth your time and effort? ("How I Became an Advertising Expert" could be a book in itself, but in the interest of time, I'll restrict myself to a few paragraphs!)

Let me begin by telling you that I never studied Advertising or Marketing in college. I'm a musician, born with the gift of communicating emotions through music. My chosen career was as a Professor of Music in the State University of New York, where I was honored to receive the prestigious *New York State Chancellor's Award for Excellence in Teaching* in 1977. Simultaneous to my teaching duties, I arranged music for several internationally acclaimed Jazz artists, and remained active in the recording studio, producing several record albums. (Funny, but the very use of the term "record album" pretty well dates me, doesn't it?) As Director of the college Jazz ensembles, I took my student musicians on concert tour every year, culminating in performances at regional Jazz festivals. I was having a pretty good time before being confronted with a harsh reality of the teaching profession. One morning, I was honored as an "excellent teacher" at a reception hosted by the college president. That same afternoon, the president invited me into his office to inform me of my retrenchment. So much for the prestigious award I had received only that morning! Mr.

President explained that the college was under extreme financial duress, and difficult decisions had to be made "for the good of the academic community." I was chosen for the honor of retrenchment because, to paraphrase the president, *you have demonstrated the ability to succeed in another field, unlike most other teachers here, who would certainly fail in the real world if retrenched. Trust me, Jeff, when you look back ten years from now, you'll understand that this was the best thing that ever happened to you.* I suppose I should have felt flattered. I didn't. Perhaps because the next day I would learn that a full 20% of the faculty had been similarly honored! (I always wondered if they all got the same *trust me* speech.) But the president's words proved prophetic. And to think I never thanked him.

After successfully convincing a banker that I knew what I was talking about even though I wasn't sure that I really did, I signed away the financial futures of my infant daughters to start a music production company. One of my first paying projects was to compose and produce a musical score for a film promoting the new School for American Craftsmen and School of Art and Design at the Rochester Institute of Technology. That film score soon became a record album that was distributed to secondary schools as a college recruitment tool. As I've told you, I never studied Advertising, and certainly nobody had ever taught me anything about what I came to know years later as Vertical Marketing, but I became obsessed with the prospect of my music not only being heard, but being performed by Jazz ensembles across the country. So, I did a little research (when I had the time), and established my own publishing company to market my musical arrangements from the film score. Although several of my compositions had already been commercially published, I wasn't too thrilled that my cut of the pie was only 10%. That alone should have been a clue that I'd eventually end up in the Advertising business! Anyway, I designed my own promotional mailing, and sent it to college and high school band directors across the United States. You can't imagine the thrill I experienced when orders started pouring in. Unfortunately, I had omitted the crucial "cost of goods sold" segment of the required research. As a result, every $25 arrangement I sold cost me $26 to market, print, package, and ship. But at least my arrangements were being performed nationwide!

It didn't take long before I was smitten with the Advertising bug. I began by producing "jingles" for some local businesses. Soon I was producing them for Advertising agencies on behalf of their clients. To be honest, I didn't even know what an ad agency was! I assumed an Advertising agency would be home to posh boardrooms, sophisticated presentations, creative conversations, and nattily dressed professionals. Nothing could have been further from reality! The ad agency executives I met were mostly cast-off radio DJ's, aspiring actors, former teachers (like me), housewives looking to get out of the house (or maybe out of the "wives"), and the usual assortment of slick operators who (thought they) could sell a refrigerator to an Eskimo. Ad agents could be found at the bottom of the "most respected business people" list, even below lawyers and car dealers! The more time I spent with these ad agency "experts," the more I realized that I seemed to have a better understanding of their clients' needs than they did. They realized it only after their clients jumped ship and hired me to handle all their Advertising needs, from soup to nuts. Suddenly, by necessity, I was a copywriter, voice talent, recording engineer, videographer, editor, producer, director, graphic artist, and media buyer, not to mention business analyst, psychological counselor, and personal guru.

In hindsight, my expectation of America's business owners was even more naïve, if that's possible. I quickly became entangled in a nationwide web of Mom-and-Pop business owners. Please don't misunderstand! Many ad agency professionals use the phrase "Mom-and-Pop" in a derogatory way. Not I! I came to develop a very deep respect for these people who made up the family and fabric of American business, probably because they were just like me...and just like you. If I could write a book about my qualifications as an

Advertising expert, I could certainly write a trilogy about some of the business owners I've met along the way! My friends (both of them) insist I should write that trilogy, and perhaps I will. For the moment, however, here's a small slice of Americana. Picture yourself walking into the office of the owner of a multimillion-dollar home furnishings store. The office was actually a converted broom closet in the basement with an art table in one corner, empty beer bottles and pizza boxes occupying the balance of available floor space. The owner and his managers engaged in a contest of which of them could "pass wind" the loudest and longest. (I "passed" on that account.) Then there was the time I accompanied my sales manager on a road trip for the purpose of pitching car dealers. *(Although you're now reading this italicized Point of Clarification in real time, I'm writing it tomorrow, some 24-hours from now. You see, I woke up in the middle of tonight with a guffaw, suddenly struck by the absurdity of our English language. What got me going was the thought of "pitching car dealers," had I used the word "pitching" in the context of playing Horse Shoes, which is not how I intended it, unfortunately. I guess writing a book is a lot like writing an ad. There's no shut-off valve. Anyway, back to the paragraph you were reading in real time. Sorry to have interrupted you.)* Meet Ed and Frank, two brothers who still owned one of the oldest Dodge dealerships in the country, somewhere out in East-who-knows-where. Ed was 90, and blind. Frank was 92, and deaf. In we walk with our TV monitor and demo tape. As the saying goes, you had to be there! But Ed and Frank turned out to have the most incredible sense of humor imaginable. Purely out of politeness, they insisted we proceed with showing the demo tape. Ed, who was blind, sat a good distance from the TV screen and picked up his battery-powered megaphone. As the tape played, Ed **shouted** every word of every commercial so Frank could hear what was going on. Meanwhile Frank, who was deaf, sat right in front of the TV screen and attempted to describe all the visuals in a way that helped Ed *see* the commercials in his mind's eye. Bedlam? You can't begin to imagine.

Within minutes everyone's ribs ached from laughter, Ed and Frank included.

I suppose I should explain what I was doing on the road, pitching car dealers, in the first place! I was wise enough to realize without being told that the "key to success" in Advertising would be the ability to syndicate my work. What is syndicate? Surely you've turned on the TV in your hotel room in Oshkosh, and seen the "same" commercial for a local car dealer that you saw weeks before in your hotel room in Peoria. It takes so much creativity and monetary resources to produce a successful ad campaign that it just makes good financial sense to sell it as many times as possible, requiring only name changes. (OK, I admit it. I'm really just lazy.) Think of it like a cookie cutter. On the assumption you've created the tastiest "master cookie" ever encountered by man or beast, the cookie cutter allows you to cut out dozens of "clone cookies" in the time it would have taken to create just one cookie without the cutter, not to mention the wasted "dough!" I soon learned that you never actually *sell* the "master cookie" to anyone, but you *license* the "clone cookies" for eating over a specified period of time. When the feast is over, and everyone is too full to eat another bite, you put the "master cookie" back on the shelf for a year or two, then reintroduce it into the marketplace when the time is right. (Unlike cookies, commercials don't get stale!) Within five years, the concept of commercial syndication had enabled me to grow my small local ad agency into a rather formidable company that was handling retail accounts throughout the Northeast. After ten years, the company boasted accounts throughout the entire United States and Canada, and housed sophisticated internal production facilities to accommodate all the work. We had video post-production suites, multitrack audio recording studios, graphic arts studio, and computer-assisted media buying department, all under one roof. Unlike traditional ad agencies, which represented their clients as third-party securers of freelance service providers, my agency did it all, in-house, from conceptualization to production to implementation to management of all campaigns.

Within fifteen years, the agency was successfully handling the Advertising activities of regional and national franchise companies, cooperative buying groups, manufacturers and trade associations. I designed and delivered educational Advertising seminars to thousands of business owners and managers at their national conventions. (More than a few TV, Radio and Newspaper executives were known to sneak in uninvited!) It wasn't unusual at any given time for the agency to have 500 different retail businesses "on the air" throughout North America, all running different Advertising campaigns. Whereas the underlying philosophy of the agency had always been to produce everything in-house to maintain strict quality control, the sheer volume of work dictated that we had no choice but farm-out work that could no longer be handled under our roof. Over and above our own facilities, we kept at least one major television production house working **Night and Day**. (Thank you, Cole Porter!) Remember me suggesting that you "throw a party at your place of business, every day"? Can you even imagine throwing 500 parties, in 500 cities, every week, at all variety of 500 car dealerships, carpet stores, furniture stores, and appliance stores? Years of such partying provided more headaches than I cared to endure, so when someone offered to buy the company, responding with "yes, please" was actually quite easy. Twenty years at the helm was more than adequate, thank you.

Remember, now, as promised I've condensed years into paragraphs, and I certainly don't mean to imply that any of this was as easy as I'm making it sound. It wasn't. I had more than my share of anxious moments, as you will in running your own business. It comes with the territory. But here I am, living in Williamsburg, Virginia, after half-a-lifetime in the infamous snow and cold of Western New York. Which brings me to the question of whether I've gained your trust, and your confidence in my ability to assist you in your efforts to make the

Advertising game work to your benefit. And make no mistake. It is a game. How well you play the game will have a major impact on the financial health of your business. So, I now ask you, are you ready to open your mind to some Advertising **Secrets** which could help make your business more successful? If so, read on. If not, just put the book back on the shelf, please!

TURN YOUR NEGATIVES INTO POSITIVES

You know you've arrived as an Advertising expert when someone calls you on the phone, and says, "I'm friends with Bill in Rochester. He's told me what a great job you've done for him, so I'd like to meet with you about doing the same for me." That's how I met Irwin. His problem was certainly not unique. Irwin's business had been in the same downtown location for many years. Unfortunately, that location was in Lackawanna, which many people not lucky enough to have been raised there referred to as "the armpit of Western New York." (Sorry, Lackawannites! I love you, though.) In better times, Lackawanna had been a thriving and prosperous community, the very heart of Western New York steel production as the home of Bethlehem Steel. But the steel mill closed down, and the town soon followed suit. While the street where Irwin had his store was undoubtedly once the main drag, now it was just a drag, with blocks of boarded-up store fronts and miles of potholes. (Interestingly enough, my wife was born and raised in nearby Buffalo, and to this day she has fond memories of traveling to Lackawanna by bus with her Nana to visit the Botanical Gardens, which are still quite beautiful.)

I arrived at Irwin's store, and we exchanged the usual pleasantries, then sat down to talk about the solution to his problem. I had learned very early on in this business that it makes sense to pay close attention to what the business owner says, because s/he usually already knows what needs to be done, but can't (or won't) vocalize it for fear of sounding silly. Irwin readily identified the problem he was facing. "This is a ghost town! Even people who live in Lackawanna don't shop here any more. So tell me, Jeff, how do we make people *wanna* come here to shop?" At this point in my narrative, I should tell you that Irwin owned a dinette specialty store. Most people didn't even know what a dinette was. (Just so you won't feel embarrassed, a dinette is what used to be referred to as a Kitchen set, you know, table and chairs, as opposed to a formal Dining Room set. Except that in recent years dinettes had become much more elegant and desirable.) As we sat and spoke that afternoon in Irwin's showroom, no less than 10 "customers" came in and asked for a cup of coffee, thinking a dinette must be some kind of a luncheonette! Irwin and I had a good laugh, dreaming up Advertising scenarios to take advantage of that confusion. "Come on in and buy your new dinette set, and while you're here, have a saaammich and a cup-a-cawwwwffee on the house." And you thought Advertising couldn't be any fun!

Eventually, the conversation turned into a debate, no, an argument about which Advertising medium would be best for the job at hand. Irwin's recent experiences, like most local retailers, had focused solely on local newspaper Advertising. Sadly, fewer and fewer people were reading the newspaper these days, especially in Lackawanna. I was able to convince Irwin that he needed to be on Radio in order to reach consumers with a little more disposable income in nearby Buffalo, as well as create the kind of excitement that would make consumers *wanna* shop in Lackawanna. Then it hit me like a ton of bricks. *"You're gonna wanna come to Lackawanna!"* Yes, that's how I earned the big bucks, fans! Simple, to the point, and it mimics exactly what Irwin had been saying for the past three hours! The next step was to create a memorable musical theme, you know, a "jingle." Can't you hear it? A sultry woman's voice, *"You're gonna wanna (pause) come to Lackawanna..."* A good old fashioned swing band kicks in with a rousing Benny Goodman-esque music bed, and a whole chorus of female vocalists sings, *"To shop Irwin's Dinette, ba-da-dee-dat-n-do-dah!"* Once he heard the jingle completed, even Irwin got excited. (That was scary.) And before you know it, with a well thought out musical framework in place, a 60-second Radio spot more or less wrote itself. All I did was let my pencil float over the page!

We hit the airwaves…heavy…on Wednesday to promote a 4-day sale on Thursday, Friday, Saturday and Sunday. Irwin was on pins and needles the entire week before his long-awaited and expensive introduction to the modern world of Radio Advertising. And I'm not ashamed to admit that I got nervous before every promotion I ever did for every client. Not because I didn't have confidence in my ability, but because there were always too many variables over which I had no control, like a few feet of snow falling in Buffalo the day of the sale. Or an event of national importance forcing the pre-emption of all local ads on Radio on the very day you've scheduled all your commercials to run! Or the Buffalo Bills losing a football game (which was a common occurrence in those days), whereby Western New York went into mourning for weeks at a time. As far as Irwin was concerned, my nervousness was proof positive that I really cared about his business, and that was important to him.

Oh, you *wanna* know the results? Irwin called me on the phone *Wednesday* evening, saying there was a big problem! My heart skipped a beat before I was finally able to ask him what was wrong. After a very pregnant pause and some heavy sighing, Irwin answered, "The problem is, Jeff, we were mobbed today, and the sale doesn't even start 'til tomorrow! This is unbelievable!" Then the chuckling started. Over the years, I would come to learn that my clients just loved to yank my chain, getting me all choked up by playing that same little Mom-and-Pop trick on me. I called it "pulling an Irwin." It never failed, and I fell for it without exception! Well, Thursday was a big day, Friday was OK (which is typical for Friday), Saturday was the biggest sales day in the history of the company, and Sunday capped it off with a bang. Yes, Irwin was back in business. For many months to follow, *"You're gonna wanna come to Lackawanna"* was literally the talk of Western New York. Radio DJ's even had on-air contests for call-in listeners, offering prizes for the best spontaneous rendition of Irwin's jingle! That's called "free PR," and you can't buy it for a million bucks.

One of the most important things you can do for your business is turn your negatives into positives. And believe me, you'll have some negatives! Let those negatives work *for* you, not against you. Irwin's "location, location, location" was a disaster. But by poking fun at it in a good-natured way, in fact drawing attention to it, we used it to our advantage instead of detriment. You can do the same, whether your negative is a "bad" location, lack of identity, newness to business, sagging economy, or any other perceived obstacle to your success. At this point, you might be thinking to yourself, "Big deal, I could have thought of that *wanna-wanna* rhyme!" And guess what. You're absolutely right! Did you really think Advertising was brain surgery or something? Furthermore, do you think this topic was the subject of any college Advertising class? I rather doubt it. Of course, what do I know, anyway? I've already told you that I never studied Advertising or Marketing in college! **Chances Are** you didn't either. (Thank you, Johnny Mathis!)

GRAB THEIR ATTENTION

At 24 years of age, Jay found himself in the position of running a major car dealership. He was by no means born with a silver spoon in his mouth. On the contrary, he started working at his father's dealership as a youngster, washing cars, changing oil, and learning every aspect of the car business from the ground up. Jay's father had successfully built his business into one of the first multi-point dealerships in the nation. At that time, if you were a car dealer, you were a single-point dealer, which means you sold Fords, or Chevrolets, or Dodges. But never two competing brands…let alone fifteen! The first time I was to meet Jay's dad would be six years later, at Jay's funeral. I confess that Jay's untimely death personally traumatized me. The memory of that day is as fresh today as the day it happened. I was awakened by my clock radio at 7:30 that morning to the sound of the commercial I had only yesterday produced for Jay's dealership. I always enjoyed hearing my commercials on the air, in the context which they would be experienced by the typical radio listener. The commercial sounded great on-air, as I had hoped it would. Next came the prerecorded newscaster's voice, "The news this morning is brought to you by…," followed by the name of Jay's dealership. That's called a sponsor audio billboard, and it was one of the perks I had successfully negotiated. By way of background, all radio commercials were transferred to "carts" (tape cartridges) for later airing. The days of cueing up reel-to-reel audio tapes were long gone. Neither the audio engineer nor the DJ had any idea what might be on any given cart, since carts were pre-logged by code number. The newscaster sat in the broadcast booth, oblivious to the carts that were being loaded in sequence by the attending engineer, and unable to hear

12

them anyway without the benefit of headphones. Immediately after Jay's commercial and billboard concluded, the newscaster received the standard finger-pointing cue from the engineer to deliver the live news headline of the morning, which on this day was the announcement of Jay's tragic death in a car accident less than eight hours before. My first wakeful thought was that this must be someone's sick idea of a joke…Jay's commercial had just aired, after all…that proves he's fine! Not knowing what else to do, I drove to the dealership, arriving at the same time as the stunned employees. Everyone was in a daze, including me. I remember walking into Jay's office, where the two of us had sat and joked the previous afternoon, enjoying the last meeting of the day. I sat in the chair that had become my place, and noticed my media proposals still sitting on his desk, waiting to be read first thing this morning. I was shaken by the sight of two half-full coffee cups still on the desk in front of me, convinced that if I just picked mine up and finished the contents, Jay would surely walk over to finish his. Who can really explain the extent of our emotions when tragedy occurs? As one of my first clients, and the first car dealer I would work with, Jay and I had quickly established a camaraderie that can only grow from the seed of mutual trust. It wasn't that we were close personal friends. Oh, we became friendly in a business kind of way, as agents and their clients often do. But he had his personal life and family, and I had mine. We didn't socialize. As I said, I met Jay's dad for the first time when I walked through the receiving line at Jay's funeral. "I was Jay's advertising agent." His father looked at me warmly, and said, "Oh, yes, Jay spoke highly of you." That's when I finally lost it. The tears didn't stop for at least a week, and the sadness is ever present, albeit diminished.

Six years prior, rumor had it that Jay was "on the outs" with the ad agency that had handled his dad's account for many years. That's not surprising, since agency/client relationships are largely based on personalities. Apparently, the personality of the agency no longer meshed with the personality of the dealership after Jay took over. Every ad agency for miles around was "pitching the account." It was a prestige account, one that could quickly elevate an agency into the very desirable position of being recognized as a leader by other large clients in the area. Or, if you fumbled the ball, you weren't likely to get another shot at stardom. You must understand, you don't just stroll into the biggest car dealership in the region, with no experience under your belt, and request a meeting with the owner. Lucky for me, nobody ever told me that! I knew I had what it took to land that account, experience or not. But how could I prove it? The only way I knew how! I locked myself in my studio for a couple of weeks and emerged with the *baddest* jingle you've ever heard, a musical marriage of Jazz and Rock now conveniently categorized as Fusion. At the time, Jazz was still looked upon with scorn as *dirty* music, and we all knew about the perversion of *sex, drugs and rock-and-roll*. The musical theme I produced was hard driving and straight forward. I relied heavily on my big-band arranging experience to create a musical presentation that built in intensity from start to finish, which is exactly what made it so appealing. It began with the electric guitar playing a simple melodic theme, soon doubled by the electric bass three octaves lower, then the drums joined the party, and at this point it really started to kick! One by one, instruments were added to the mix…piano, sax section, screaming brass, and finally the singers belting out the lyrical theme. By the end of sixty seconds, you couldn't help but *feel* the power. For the climactic ending, I confess to borrowing an idea from my favorite musical group of the day, *Blood Sweat & Tears*. Remember the song, *More and More,* from their first album? At the very end, the entire band is holding that last note for effect. Everyone cuts off abruptly, leaving only the lead trumpet player defiantly holding an unbelievably high note for one extra second, and then he *kisses off* with a brassy *Yeowww!* (Thank you, Lew Soloff.) I was so in awe of the talent in that group, that's exactly how I ended the jingle. Radio listeners actually waited for that ending, and many told me they always got the goose bumps…from a commercial! Can you tell that I believe musical presentation can be key to a great ad? In the early stages of my Advertising career, music was my admission to the game, so to speak. It opened many doors. With the musical framework in place, I conceptualized what I thought would be a great campaign, wrote some sample ad copy, and produced a series of radio commercials. This is called "spec" work, short for speculative. You do it at your own expense, in the hope it gets you in the door for a meeting. Very few ad agents did spec work, mostly because it was expensive, and there was no guarantee it would get you anywhere. But what did I know? I had the luxury, no, burden, of owning my own little recording studio, so it really didn't cost me anything but time. And I was confident it would not only get me in the door, but would help me land that first big account.

Casual as could be, I walked through the front door of the dealership and approached the elevated sales podium, which was by now standard in most car dealerships. It was essential that the sales manager maintain the negotiating advantage of looking down at you from on high! Big Vince greeted me with a grunt. "Yeah, waddaya want?" (By the way, Big Vince was true to his name. I came to know him over the years as a gentle soul, but *puleeeeeze* don't tell him I said that.) "I'd like to see the owner, please." Vince scowled down over the podium with a look of disdain. "Waddaya wanna see 'im for? He's verrrry busy." In hindsight, I can't blame Vince for guarding the gate. There I stood, bushy full-face beard, curly mop of hair down to my shoulders, wearing jeans and sneakers. But at least I had my tweed sport coat on! I nonchalantly lifted up my oversized boom-box, and pointed to the cassette tape that was loaded and ready to play. "This is your next ad campaign," I boasted. "Is that so?" Vince bellowed. "I'll tellya whad," he challenged. "Play it for me first, and if I like it maybe I'll play it for the owner." Not one to be shy when it comes to my music, I pressed the Play button, and turned the volume up full blast. For that first moment, Vince actually allowed his nervousness at the volume level to show, even though *he* was the one on the podium! After all, there were customers in the showroom. Within 30-seconds, no less than a dozen people formed a tight semi-circle around us at the podium. When my spec commercials finished playing, everyone not only applauded, but they asked to hear the tape again. "Wait here," Vince ordered. A minute or two later, Jay came out of his office, introduced himself and shook hands, inviting me in for a cup of coffee. I almost laughed out loud, thinking about the conversations Irwin and I had enjoyed only weeks earlier about "Come in and have a saaaaammich and a cup of cawwwwfee." I managed to stifle the laugh, and replayed my spec commercials for Jay. "Who did these?" he demanded. "I did," I answered. "This is good stuff...*really* good." Coming from Jay, that was the ultimate compliment. "Thank you," I replied. That day, I was appointed ad agency of record. I guess I was successful in grabbing Jay's attention. The title of this chapter is actually meant to convey the necessity of grabbing the consumer's attention. But as an ad agent, you can't very well grab the consumer's attention until you've first grabbed the business owner's attention!

The above mentioned meeting occurred in 1980. If you were around then, you may recall that interest rates were at about 17%. (I know, because my wife and I had just bought our first house!) Car dealerships were dropping like flies, because people were holding on to their cars for as long as possible, unable to afford the finance charges on a new one. As a result, sticker prices skyrocketed, adding the unpleasant element of "sticker shock," a new American phenomenon. I had an idea what it must be costing Jay in "floor plan" bank interest charges to maintain such a monumental inventory of vehicles across 15 franchises. In fact, I suspect the monthly electric bill at his dealership was higher than my annual earnings. I was bold enough to ask him how the economy was affecting his business. "We're still here!" he replied with a shrug. At no other time in recent history was it more imperative that you not only grab the consumer's attention, but motivate him/her to shop at your place of business, immediately, lest s/he lose out on a spectacular offering that may never be repeated (until next week). While meeting with new clients, it was my habit to stroll around the building, taking in the feel of the place. I noticed dozens of pairs of roller skates hanging from the ceiling. I asked Jay about this, and he told me he had recently acquired a controlling interest in a business that manufactured the skates. To my right as we sat in Jay's office was a red brick wall. My reason for mentioning these two seemingly meaningless and unrelated facts will soon become clear.

The campaign theme that I conceptualized for Jay's dealership in my spec commercials was *The World's Greatest Car Dealer.* After all, what more could you say about a dealership housing 15 different franchises? The first major promotional event I produced for Jay was *The World's Greatest Car Sale.* (Over the next few years, this event would be syndicated to over 300 car dealers across the country, and was voted "The Most Outstanding Promotion in America.") The real beauty of the event, from the perspective of the dealership, is that not once did it refer to price, financing, or monthly payments! No, we were selling the excitement of the event, which was called "hype." This was crucial to the financial success of the event to the dealer, since he didn't have to "give the store away" to attract the consumers' attention. As with any successful promotion, you need a "hook." At about the 40-second mark of my radio commercial, I hit 'em with the right hook! (Pun intended.) *"Listen…if you don't buy from us today…you may as well roller skate home, bang your head against a brick wall, and forget about a car for another year!"* Recognize those two seemingly unrelated and meaningless facts? Once again, that's why I got the big bucks! This became known as the *slap-em-in-the-face* style of advertising, combining the raw power of the music with the dramatic delivery of an inspiring announcer (me), designed to give the consumer no choice but to listen *and* respond. We introduced *The World's Greatest Car Sale* my first month on the account. Talk about being thrown to the wolves! The right hook delivered the desired knockout, while conveying a certain perverse sense of humor about the economy. Over a four-day time span, the dealership sold more vehicles than they had sold in the previous four weeks. Pretty good start!

Over the next six years, we would develop many such successful events, all variations on the original *World's Greatest* theme. In fact, a pattern developed. We would typically launch a new event on the radio on Thursday, leading into strong weekend sales. It became habit for me to visit the dealership every Tuesday, cassette tape in hand, to play the upcoming weekend's radio commercial I had just completed, for Jay's approval. And it became Jay's habit to invite Big Vince and any available salesmen to take a seat in a new van on the showroom floor, into which we would all squeeze, for the purpose of listening to the tape. As you might expect, Big Vince always took up the seat furthest to the rear...*all* of it. We would play the commercial repeatedly, and everyone would have their chance to say "yay or nay." (In six years, I never heard a "nay.") I always enjoyed working with car dealers because their sense of humor was usually as wicked as mine! I put that wickedness to the ultimate test on one occasion, and I'll never forget it. It was Tuesday, the day of our eagerly awaited in-the-van listening session at Jay's dealership. But on this Tuesday, I had to fly to some distant city to deliver a seminar. I called Jay before I left, explaining why I wouldn't be able to make our meeting that day, but promised him I would make it the next day, Wednesday. Jay understood, but expressed a little concern over not being able to approve the radio commercial until the day before it was to air. "What if I don't like it, Jeff?" As I said, I hadn't yet heard a "nay," and that's when the idea hit me. I told Jay not to worry, if he didn't like it I would stay up all night Wednesday, if necessary, to produce one he liked. Actually, I did stay up all night, but not Wednesday.

When I returned from my seminar at midnight Tuesday, I drove straight from the airport to my recording studio and devoted three hours to producing the most...well...*obscene* radio commercial you could imagine. The first ten seconds sounded like any other of our commercials, with the standard *World's Greatest* opening: *"Today…the sun will rise at noon…for the World's Greatest…"* But from that point on, I must admit it got pretty raunchy, so much so that I'm a little embarrassed to continue the above recitation of the script. (Oh, all right, if you insist on a hint, substitute the word "son" for "sun" and imagine the rest!) Late Wednesday afternoon, I arrived at the dealership prepared for our much-anticipated listening session. As usual, the van filled to overflow…I think they had started charging for admission…with Big Vince holding down the rear, so to speak. With as straight a face as I could manage, I explained to Jay that I had already anticipated his approval of the commercial he was about to hear, and had sent the master tape to the radio stations for broadcast the next morning. As much as Jay trusted my judgment, I couldn't help but notice the slight rise of his left eyebrow. I placed the cassette tape in the van's tape player and pressed the Play button, sliding the volume up to full as required. During the first ten seconds, everyone settled back into their seats comfortably, appreciating what had become the standard opening to our commercials. And then the fun started, at least for me. At first, there was stunned silence on the part of the vansters. Then, word by word, the laughter started, ever so slowly. By the end of the commercial, Big Vince had the van rocking precariously from left to right, front to back. Looking out the van windows, we could see customers and salesmen alike staring in astonishment, wondering what kind of drunken brawl could possibly be taking place inside the van. "Play it again, Jeff" was repeated no less than a dozen times. When we were finally all laughed out, our departure from the van must have resembled a scene from the circus, a seemingly endless processional of red-faced clowns filing out from the one open van door. Everyone just stood and stared, jaws dropped in amazement. And then, just when you were absolutely convinced not one more body could possibly have been squeezed into that van…out tumbled Big Vince, hiking up his drawers! Once outside in fresher air, Jay pulled me aside and asked, "You didn't really send that tape to the stations, did you, Jeff?" I had no choice but to answer "Of course I did…why, don't you like it?" I got another raised eyebrow, this one the right, and Jay made sure I didn't leave without giving him the tape. "You're kidding," I protested. "Just give me the tape, Jeff!" So, I did. As had become my habit, I showed up at the dealership late Saturday afternoon to see how the promotion was going. Oh, the place was rockin', as they say. And you'll never guess what was playing through the loudspeakers at maximum volume, not only *in* the dealership, but *outside* on the sales lots. Yep, you guessed it. The joke was now on me. Just as "pulling an Irwin" had become a practice to be expected, so too did my new game of "pulling a Jeff!" Looking back, I think new clients were actually attracted to my agency by the masochistic anticipation of being victimized at the most inopportune moment by that now legendary "pull." Wait a minute, now, don't look at me like that. I told you those car dealers were really a bad influence! I must admit, though, I really do miss those days.

You must grab the consumer's attention before you can expect to be recognized. You can do this in your ads by incorporating humor, music, special offers, slogans, celebrity spokesperson, your own version of *slap-'em-in-the-face* aggressiveness, even sex appeal. You'll find the approach most appropriate for your situation. Fail to grab attention and **Watch What Happens**. (Thank you, Michel LeGrand!) Absolutely nothing.

CREATE SOME MAGIC

Tony had a very big mountain to climb! After many years as an upper level manager for a regional chain of stores, he went off on his own and opened a small store, eager to put his skills to work for himself. Perhaps like you, Tony had a dream of doing things differently, of doing them better. It's one thing to manage an established and proven group of stores for someone else. It's another thing entirely to start from ground zero with your own store, as Tony soon realized. But there he was, forced to compete with his former boss for his very economic survival. His dilemma seemed insurmountable. How do you successfully play David to a Goliathan chain of stores that had a virtual stranglehold on the marketplace? How do you go head to head with a conglomerate that could outspend you in Advertising by at least twenty-to-one? What could you say about your new store that hadn't already been said about all the other similar stores in the city, of which there must have been dozens? Simply put, how do you create some magic at your store? This is the challenge faced by all new business owners, and the one that stared Tony in the eye from Day One. Tony invited me into his nightmare, and I shared the challenge that confronted him. I had no illusions about the task at hand. It would be up to me to find a niche Tony could fill, quickly and inexpensively. What else is new, right? I knew we couldn't outspend the competition. In fact, Tony's annual Advertising budget was probably the equivalent of one weekend's budget for his former boss. We had to find a way to make an impact without breaking the bank. To put it another way, we had to throw a fun party that would create some magic at Tony's new store!

Mike was one of the most interesting characters I've ever met! He parked himself on my agency doorstep one morning and said he wanted to work for me. Mike was young, a college dropout, and had no experience in the Advertising industry, but he was passionate about learning the ropes. I had no idea where to put Mike, so I invited him to "hang around" for awhile, to see if this was what he really wanted to do with the rest of his life. Mike jumped at the chance, and the next few months found him trying his hand at all variety of Advertising duties. We quickly learned that Mike wasn't a copywriter. And Mike wasn't an effective salesperson. He had no interest in the drudgery of media research, and no patience for the required negotiations. He wasn't technically adept, and found the recording studio boring. He wasn't a graphic artist. In fact, even his handwriting was illegible! We found countless other things Mike couldn't do. But there was one thing he could do. He could make people laugh. Mike was one of these guys who could have you in stitches at the drop of a hat, and our offices were suddenly filled with uncontrollable laughter on a daily basis. Mike had a quick wit, and the uncanny ability to cut right to the heart of any situation with a humorous remark. Personally, I had trouble being in the same room with Mike for more than a few minutes. Not because I didn't like him, but because he could get me laughing so hard that tears would roll down my cheeks and my sides would ache for hours after only minutes in Mike's presence. Maybe you know someone like Mike.

Tony was Italian. It's been said that many Italians look Jewish. Tony didn't. Mike was Jewish. It's been said that many Jews look Italian. Mike didn't. Tony was heavy. Mike was skinny. Tony was tall. Mike was short. Tony was dark. Mike was light. Tony never laughed. Mike never stopped. Tony was a man of few words. Mike never shut up! Tony had no sons. Mike had no father. I could feel it coming, another one of those big-bucks ideas! Mike was as desperate to succeed in the Advertising business as Tony was to succeed in his new business. And then it hit me, the solution to both their problems staring us in the face. Mike would get his shot at instant stardom, while Tony would get his essential Advertising "hook!" Tony would now have a son, and Mike would now have a father, at least in the make-believe world of Television Advertising. An unforgettable ad campaign was born of necessity, *"My son, the college graduate."*

The first in a series of TV commercials found Mike whispering conspiratorially to the camera, smiling out of one side of his mouth. In the background, you could see Tony, clipboard in hand, busily attending to the duties of logging his store's obviously overstocked inventory. Mike began, "That's my boss. Just look at him, 30 years in business and he still doesn't get it. I keep tellin' him, 'Boss, you need to mark this stuff down before people are gonna buy it,' and he just smiles and keeps doin' what he's doin' without answering me!" The camera cuts to a close-up of Tony, knowingly shaking his head as he overhears Mike's conspiracy-in-the-making, mumbling to himself over Mike's obvious inexperience in the ways of the business world. Mike continues, "Look at all this stuff! It's not gonna sell itself! If I was the boss, I'd mark it all down…way down…then, I'd give a free bonus with every purchase, and I'd finance my customers for a whole year, interest-free, and I'd…" At this point, Tony walks into the camera's field of vision, smiles, puts his arm around Mike's shoulder, and says with a combined sense of pride and chagrin, "My son, the college graduate." Mike responds with the guilty look of a little kid who just got caught with his hand in the cookie jar.

You'll notice that the commercial never made any reference to whether a customer would actually be offered any of the things Mike listed! It didn't have to. What we were "selling" wasn't just a product, but a family situation no different from that faced by any family, anywhere in America. And it clicked. You may find this as hard to believe as I did at the time, but people who had known Tony for 30 years called him on the phone and said, "Tony, I didn't know you had a son!" Even better, customers came into the store, and *demanded* to be waited on by Mike.

It seems they wanted their crack at the brash youngster, to say nothing of the deals he would be so apt to offer without his "father's" knowledge. Tony's standard response became, "I'm sorry, he's back at college. The only time I see him these days is when he shows up to film a new commercial!" As with any good ad campaign, the beauty of this one was that there was never a shortage of family scenarios that were credible offshoots of that first commercial. Each week found Tony and Mike in a new situation, with a new problem to solve, Mike incessantly instructing his old boss what to do and how to do it, and Dad always putting son in his place ever so gently with that classic closing line. Sure enough, Tony's business began to grow, and Mike became a star on the local airwaves. But his greatest claim to fame was summed up when one day Mike spoke these words to me in confidence, which I can now break. "The chicks really love me now!" OK, Mike!

There's an old saying, *Be careful what you wish for.* After a couple of years, Tony decided he was more comfortable as an upper level manager for someone else than as the owner of his own store. And his former boss realized it would be far less expensive to buy out the competition than compete with it, so he bought Tony's business and placed him in his former position of running the chain's stores, including the newest addition to the family. Meanwhile, Mike realized that he no longer had any interest in working in the Advertising industry. Besides, he was having trouble keeping up with all the chicks in his little black book. At least that's what he told me. The last I heard about Mike, he had moved to somewhere in Ohio. I think about Mike often, and I sincerely hope he has found a career as a stand-up comic. More likely, however, he's a practicing Psychiatrist!

We created some real magic at that store. And you can create some magic at yours. The hardest part is recognizing where it might be hiding, and what to do with it once you find it. It doesn't have to be expensive magic, either. The TV commercials we produced with Tony and Mike were not fancy or slick in any way. No makeup artists, no rehearsals, and only a couple of hours of camera and editing time were the norm. But they *were* magic, perhaps because Tony and Mike were so **Easy To Love!** (Thanks again, Cole Porter!)

CONCENTRATE YOUR EFFORTS

Roger was an account executive at a TV station in New Haven, CT. Familiar with my work, he had the good sense to invite me to New Haven to meet with one of the station's clients who "needed help." As it later turned out, the client who needed help didn't want any, which is undoubtedly why he needed it in the first place! So Roger did what any smart account executive would do...he went to the competition, a business owner named Herb who had never advertised on TV. Herb told Roger he would like to meet me. After all, I was the proverbial "expert from out of town!" My wife and I were in Albany, NY, the following week, so we hopped an Amtrak and ended up in New Haven in the midst of their worst blizzard on record. I remember the midnight train-ride well because it was so cold the toilets froze up and couldn't be used. Plus, the heating system was frozen to the core, and the unpleasant combination of cold and no bathrooms...well, you get the picture. The glamour of the Advertising world! I can only wonder how many Madison Avenue big shots have stories like this!

We had a very pleasant meeting with Herb and his daughter, son, son-in-law, brother, and brother-in-law, all key players in their family-owned furniture and appliance store, a tried and true Mom-and-Pop since 1921! But what made the meeting pleasant was much more than the fact that we ended up doing business together. We just hit it off, in a personal way. 25 years my senior, Herb became a close personal friend, introducing me as "his find" to countless business people who would eventually become my clients. Years later, his son Steve would seek me out for career advice after this family business was eventually sold. Times were tough, not only in Connecticut, but all across the country.

Consumer confidence was in the dumpster, interest rates were astronomical, and big box "category killers" were indeed killing Mom-and-Pops who just couldn't compete with the selection and volume pricing "the big boys" could offer. Unfortunately, this was the time in the history of American business that consumers gladly sacrificed service after the sale for a lower price at the time of sale. The reality of the situation was that Herb's 50,000 square foot building had to justify its financial existence, regardless of the sagging economic climate. And I won't even mention the millions of dollars worth of furniture and appliance inventory already on the books. (Oops, I just did.)

In a theme certain to recur throughout this book, Herb's previous Advertising efforts had been limited exclusively to his local newspaper, as was the tradition for Mom-and-Pops throughout the country. Don't get me wrong, I have nothing against the newspaper, but when *anything* stops working, you better find a different way to skin the cat. By the end of the meeting, I had convinced Herb and family that they needed to try something new…Television. And this was no easy task, their store being located in the middle of two major media markets, Hartford and New Haven, which is another way of saying "ads here ain't cheap!" Somewhere along the way, I had learned that most Advertising "experts" approached their clients with this infamous question: "How much can you spend?" I asked a much different question: "How much business are you and your staff capable of writing?" From there, the discussion always had a way of going where I wanted it to go. I then asked Herb how much business they wrote on the best day they ever had. After hemming and hawing, he threw a figure at me. I worked the numbers in my head quickly. A common rule of thumb for furniture retailers is that in order to consider a sale successful, you must achieve sales of at least ten times the Advertising investment over the duration of the sale. So I took Herb's number, divided it by ten, and asked myself if the resulting figure made sense in the marketplace, based on the population, which in turn determined Advertising rates! As usual, I had done my homework, and I had a pretty good idea of what was real and what wasn't. As is happens, the number Herb had quoted me for his best written sales day ever was exactly ten times what I had estimated as the cost of one solid day of TV Advertising in this market, so I immediately knew we were at least in the ballpark. I told Herb how much money he needed to invest on TV for an effective one-day sales event, based on my preliminary research. I then explained my sincere belief that if he would commit to that figure, I felt reasonably sure that the worst case scenario was that they would *only* match the best day they had ever experienced to this point! The best case scenario would be that they could double it. Herb expressed his first doubt, which was actually a fear. "Jeff, to be honest with you, we haven't had a day like that in years. I just don't know if the market is there to do those kinds of numbers." I answered the only way I knew how, with honesty. "Herb, if you're not willing to try something a little different at this point, you might as well just close your doors and give up. I honestly believe this is what you need to do, and I wouldn't recommend it to you unless I was confident that it would work." Herb thought for a moment, struggling to hide the pained look from his face. His next question was expected: "But why would you recommend that we blow our entire wad on one day, and only on Television? Wouldn't it make more sense to spread that money out over, let's say, a week, and buy some radio and newspaper, too?" I knew that most ad agents would respond to this question with the pat answer: "Sure, we'll spend your money however you want, and get you the most bang for the buck possible." My answer must have floored him. "Herb, that would be the biggest mistake you could ever make. It would dilute your effectiveness to the point where I wouldn't be able to look you in the face the next day. If that's what you decide to do, I will respectfully decline your business, and I would frankly recommend that you'd be far better off taking the money and going on vacation instead of wasting it on an Advertising campaign that is doomed to fail before it even starts." Herb stroked his chin as the family looked on in silence, and finally asked, "Will you guarantee the results?" I had only one answer: "No. You know as well as I do there are no guarantees in business. But I will guarantee you my best effort, and the down side risk is minimal, since we both know that the worst thing that could happen is you'll have a slow day and only recoup your Advertising investment. The way I see it, Herb, I've made your decision very easy." Herb looked me straight in the eye, and asked for the names and phone numbers for the owners of three furniture stores whom he could call that very minute for verification of my credentials. He thought he was scaring me by insisting I sit there and listen to his conversations over the speakerphone. I couldn't help but smile. I sat quietly. Two calls later, Herb said, "OK, let's do it!"

It's only fair to tell you that the TV budget I proposed for Herb's 1-day sale was five times what he was used to spending on a full week's worth of ads in his local newspaper. That doesn't mean TV is more expensive than newspaper, it just means that it reaches a much larger audience. And audience is what you're really paying for. If I was right (which I was), Herb and his staff could easily accommodate the increase in store traffic to justify investing so much money for one day of Advertising on TV. So, we hit the TV airwaves heavy on Friday, announcing our one-day sale on Saturday. During our Monday-morning-after-the-sale phone conversation, as I warned you would be the case, Herb "pulled an Irwin" on me. Yep, I fell for it. "Oh man, Jeff, I don't know how to tell you this, but we did everything just like you told us and…well, maybe I shouldn't tell you, but…well…no, you don't want to know…do you?" Heart pounding, I screamed, "You're damned right I want to know!" Herb couldn't contain his laughter for another moment, and all I could decipher was the phrase "we did twenty-five times our investment!" Then I heard Herb's entire family in the background, laughing and applauding! The real kicker was that business on the next day, Sunday, resulted in sales figures many times greater than the typical Sunday, despite the fact that the ads clearly indicated the sale was for one day only, Saturday. That's called residual business. It's also called a blessing.

There are many lessons to be learned here, but the most important one is the need to concentrate your efforts. It would have been far too easy to allow Herb to spread my recommended media budget over a longer period of time, with a little bit of newspaper here, a hint of TV there, and a pinch of radio somewhere else. And that would have doomed the sale to certain failure. Is it better to dilute your efforts in several media over a longer period of time, or to concentrate your efforts over a shorter period of time in one medium? **Hush Now, Don't Explain.** (Thank you, Billie Holiday!)

LISTEN TO EVERYONE

During my first few months in business, before I became (recognized as) an Advertising Expert, I spent countless hours both on the telephone and on my weary legs, trying to cold-call my way into meeting with business owners who I thought could benefit, financially, from my talents and skills. To my utter amazement, the standard answer was, "Not interested." *Click*. I know you're not supposed to take business rejection personally, and the one thing I would change about myself, if I could, would be the ability to take rejection not as a personal affront, but as a standard means of deflecting an undesired interruption. But whenever I got *clicked*, I would call right back, asking the offending *clicker*, "Why were you just so rude to me?" More often than not, I'd get *clicked* a second time. But every once in a while, I would succeed in securing an invitation to the desired meeting. On those occasions where I aroused enough curiosity to get me in the door, the standard precondition of the meeting was, "OK, you've got five minutes, then you're out of here!" I knew I had those accounts in my pocket, because the five-minute appointment *always* ended up lasting five hours. What I didn't understand about the *clickers* was why they wouldn't at least answer with the desired "you've got five minutes." After all, maybe I had something to offer that they needed, but they would never know it since they were too stupid…sorry, too busy to meet with me! Oh, well, ignorance is bliss. I spent my days watching TV, listening to the radio, and scanning the newspaper, studying and analyzing all the commercials and ads. Didn't these *clickers* understand that I could, in five minutes or less, tell them everything they were doing wrong? I guess not. The whole point is that everyone has something to offer, and unless and until you're willing to listen, you may just end up missing out on that one-in-a-million idea that someone (like me) stumbles over on his way into your office! Talk is cheap, and it costs nothing to listen. You never know what you may hear, but only if you're listening. So, I continued pounding the pavement, searching for good listeners.

My own listening skills were put to the test the day I received a phone call from Henry, an established ad agent in town. "You listen to me, you rotten little son-of-a-b____! Don't you *ever* pitch one of my clients again! Who the f___ do you think you are, anyway?" That was just Henry's way of saying hello. He rambled on for a good fifteen minutes, reading me the riot act. I was too stunned to speak up in my defense, so I just listened. Besides, my heart felt like it would soon beat out of my chest, so I pressed the phone's mute button and did some deep breathing exercises while Henry vented. When it was obvious he had tired himself out, having depleted all the four-letter words in his vocabulary (which was quite extensive), he paused, perhaps just to make sure I had been listening, whereupon I released the mute button and *very* calmly and softly answered, "Thanks for calling." That must have taken him back a step or two, because he actually answered me with a courteous "You're welcome." Not for a moment doubting the pen was mightier than the sword, I immediately sat down at my typewriter (no computers yet, remember?) and composed this letter of response, which I mailed to Henry that same afternoon:

Dear Henry,

Thank you so much for your kind phone call today. I have enclosed a list of my current accounts, all six of them, complete with the names and phone numbers of the owners. I encourage you to call each of them, and take your best shot. If you succeed, I will not have lost an account, you will have won an account. In the interest of keeping the peace, I will update you on the 30th day of each month with a similar listing of all my new accounts for your review.

Yours truly,
Jeff

I followed through on my promise of monthly updates to Henry for the next year, by which time the list had grown to include clients in several cities. I don't know that Henry ever actually called any of my clients. Perhaps he should have, because a year later he called me again, this time to explain that his agency had gone bust and could I use some help. I thanked him for the courtesy of the call, and invited him in to meet with me in my office. You're probably thinking I hired Henry, but such was not the case. I just didn't think he had the necessary ingredients to help me grow my agency…but at least I extended him the courtesy of listening to what he had to say. Frankly, it's not only courteous, it's the smart thing to do.

By no means am I suggesting that every idea presented will be that one-in-a-million gem in the rough. If you're lucky enough to get one in your life, it was still worth the time invested. I can immediately think of one gem I was rewarded with, just for listening. I had just licensed *The*

World's Greatest Car Sale (see **Grab Their Attention**) to Joe, a car dealer in Buffalo, NY. Early one morning, weeks before the event was even scheduled to run at his dealership, Joe called me on the phone to tell me that I'd be receiving a call from a gentleman named Lewis. He wouldn't tell me why Lewis would be calling me, he just said to be sure to listen to what Lewis had to say. Sure enough, about an hour later, Lewis called, introducing himself as the *World's Greatest Syndicator of Advertising for Car Dealers*. That certainly got my attention, since I had aspirations of securing that very same title! Not knowing that Joe had already warned me to expect this call, Lewis went on to explain that he had just made a sales presentation to a car dealer (Joe) in Buffalo, hoping to sell Joe one of his syndicated campaigns. Apparently, Joe told Lewis that he had only days earlier licensed *The World's Greatest Car Sale* from me. Joe still had my demo tape, which he showed to Lewis. "I have never, in all my years in this business," continued Lewis, "seen anything as well done as the event Joe showed me on your reel. I'm only 70 miles from you, and I'm on my way over to meet with you right this moment, as I'm flying out tonight. Now understand, Jeff, I have never sold anyone else's work, only my own, but I want to sell yours! Frankly, it's the best I've seen, and I've seen it all. I guarantee I can sell it for more money than you're selling it for!" Again, Lewis had my attention. Despite the fact that I'd met a lot of *refrigerator salesmen* in this business, I reminded myself that it couldn't hurt to listen, so I invited Lewis to come on over for lunch, which he did. Lewis was indeed an interesting character, full of bluster and a little too bombastic for my style, but he was quite the salesman. The first question he asked me during our lunch was, "How much are you selling this campaign for?" I wasn't going to fall into that trap, so I answered his question with my own, "How much would *you* sell it for?" He answered my question with his, "How much commission are you prepared to pay me?" I answered that question with another, "How much do you want?" He answered with yet another, "Have you ever paid anyone 50% commission?" He had me there, and I replied, simply,

"Nope, never have." Lewis then dropped a dollar figure of what he thought he could get for my event. I did my best not to let my jaw hit the floor, since the figure he quoted was a full five times what I was licensing it for. Quick mental gymnastics revealed that even if I paid him 50% of each sale, if he could in fact sell my event for five times what I was selling it for currently, I'd still end up getting at least two-and-a-half times more than I was getting, even after paying him his 50%! With nothing to lose but the cost of lunch, I inked a deal with Lewis. We drove back to my office, and I provided Lewis with the necessary demonstration materials, wondering if I would ever hear from him again. Three days later, he mailed in his first order. True to his promise, the check from Lewis' licensing dealer was exactly five times what I had been selling my event for. True to mine, I sent Lewis a check for his 50%. The next day, I received order number two, this time for eight times my former price. And so it went. I wish I could tell you our business relationship continued for many years, but it didn't. A couple of years later, all contact from Lewis just stopped, dead in the water. I actually thought something might have happened to him, or that he was ill, so I tried calling, writing, faxing, to no avail. Years later, I would accidentally stumble upon Lewis' web site, and what to my wondering eyes do I behold but my very own *World's Greatest Car Sale*. Only it wasn't displayed under my copyright, it was presented in its full glory as Lewis' own creation. Apparently, Lewis was no longer satisfied with a mere 50% cut of my pie, and had decided 100% was more to his liking! That mistake prompted a lovely little letter from my attorney, "requesting" that he immediately desist. Copyright violation is a serious crime, and the penalties are substantial.

In spite of any unpleasant lessons like the one I learned from Lewis, I encourage you to listen to all ideas from all sources. Advertising agencies are in the business of conceiving ideas. Whether you decide to hire an agent is not the issue. But if someone is willing to give you some ideas, like I always did, why not listen? As I explained in **Grab Their**

Attention, I often went into first meetings armed to the hilt with spec commercials, music, newspaper layouts, whatever I thought it would take to land an account. Even on smaller accounts that might not have financially justified such elaborate advance preparation, I was always eager to share my thoughts and ideas with business owners. That's what the Advertising business is all about, after all. As my agency grew, adding more accounts each month than most other agencies secured in a year, I always *encouraged* my clients to remain receptive to meeting with other agents and listening to their ideas. In fact, I *insisted* on it. Every once in a while, one of my clients would tell me about an idea that had been presented to him in just such a meeting with a competing agency, and would ask how I might improve upon it. I can tell you that no client ever left me for want of a better idea. No, **You Can't Take That Away From Me.** (Thanks, George Gershwin!)

BEES AND HONEY

Lynn was the first employee I hired at my fledgling company, other than my wife, who worked without pay! At the time, Lynn was employed at a local TV station as Traffic Manager, which is a fancy title for someone who makes sure everyone else completes their assigned duties in a timely manner. It was Lynn's responsibility to maintain daily contact with all the local advertisers and their agencies to make sure their commercials were in the station's production vaults, properly logged, scheduled, and ready for airing. It's probably the most thankless job at the station, as well as the lowest paying. Given that a vast majority of business owners often prefer to ignore the details they don't care to bother with, to say nothing of their agents, the Traffic Manager needs to be both firm and polite, so as not to offend a customer. And if anyone ever makes a mistake, it always falls on the Traffic Manager's shoulders, since that position holds up the bottom of the station totem pole. As a young agency supplying a steady flow of commercials to that TV station on behalf of a growing stable of local clients, I spoke with Lynn on a daily basis by telephone. I was most impressed with her general demeanor, and the way she conscientiously handled the responsibilities of her position. To be more precise, she was always efficient and pleasant, a rare combination of talents that added up to the definition of a professional, in my book. So, when I recognized the agency's need for a *Chief Cook and Bottle Washer,* I called Lynn and invited her to meet with me to discuss the possibility of leaving her job at the TV station in favor of a more glamorous career in Advertising. She accepted the invitation, and the job. Looking back, hiring Lynn was unquestionably the wisest business decision I ever made. As I suspected might be the case, she turned out to be one of those rare individuals who would do whatever was required to help the agency grow and prosper, even if it wasn't part of her job description. Oh, she had a fault, maybe even two! A college graduate with a degree in English, Lynn couldn't spell to save her life! (Sorry, Lynn.) Even worse, no one could read her atrocious handwriting! But both problems were solved with the advent of the personal computer and spell-check.

Literally her first day on the job, I had to fly to New Jersey for a major new client presentation. Without a second thought, I left Lynn in charge of the fort. Years later, she would confide that she almost quit that first day on the job! She was besieged with phone calls, questions she had no idea how to answer, and a host of deadlines that I had failed to warn her about before departing. Lucky for me, she hung in there that first day, and for years to follow. My wife and I came to regard Lynn as our third daughter, and our daughters thought of her as Auntie Lynnie. She proved eager to learn about every aspect of the business, and performed each task with the same sense of diligence and purpose. When work needed to get done, she stayed late, or arrived early. As our staff grew, Lynn became a mentor and seemed to be able to solve any problem before it became one. Remember meeting Mike in **Create Some Magic?** If you recall, I said that we found countless things Mike couldn't do before discovering the one thing he did best, which was making people laugh. In Lynn's case, we found so many things she could do, and do well, that it was difficult to define what she did best, which was simply to be herself. Everyone liked her, from clients to vendors to coworkers. Ask her a question and you knew you would get a straight answer, with never an excuse or a complaint.

You may be wondering why I'm telling you about Lynn. After all, she wasn't a client with an experience I could turn into a chapter in my book! However, I'll let you in on a little secret. I proudly admit that I learned a very important lesson from her, which I'll now share with you. Take it to heart, and you'll save yourself years of agony in your negotiating strategy with vendors, Advertising reps, and even customers. In the beginning stages of my agency's development, I personally handled all media negotiations with TV and Radio stations on behalf of my clients. As a young businessman on the grow, with a rapidly increasing client list, which resulted in a substantial flow of Advertising dollars being allocated to those stations, I admit I probably got at least a little bit caught up in my own sense of self-importance. Although those who knew me on a personal basis, away from the office, had no doubt that I was really a pretty mellow kind of guy, when it came to negotiating media expenditures with station account executives and their managers, I was, shall we say, forceful. I took my position as caretaker of my clients' money to heart, and I made no excuses about demanding what I expected to receive from the stations in exchange for my clients' hard-earned Advertising dollars. If my clients' needs weren't met to my satisfaction, I felt no hesitation whatsoever in making my displeasure known to station management, or anyone else who might be expected to cave in to my demands. I can remember ruining at least one business lunch by getting up and departing in a huff, angry that my wishes weren't being taken seriously by those in attendance! (In truth, I don't think it ruined lunch. The restaurant took care of that!)

I gained the respect of my clients by getting the biggest media bang possible for their bucks. As the agency continued to grow, however, I recognized the need to start training someone else in the fine art of media negotiations. Lynn stepped up to the plate and asked me to pitch her the ball, which I did. I spent countless weeks trying to instill the necessity of being a tough negotiator, and I gave her the required tools to earn her new title of *Chief Cook and Media Buyer*. The more I coached, the more we both realized a leopard just can't discard her spots, no matter how hard she tries! I admit, I was beginning to have serious doubts about Lynn's future as a media negotiator. I feared she just wasn't mean enough, or tough enough, or vindictive enough to succeed in this demanding and competitive arena. Despite my apprehension, she politely invited me to "chill out" and let her take her own swing at the ball without me constantly hovering over her shoulder, which I agreed to do.

Over the course of the next few weeks, Lynn assumed more and more of the agency's media negotiating responsibilities. Watching from a distance, I noticed that despite the pressures of the job, she was always smiling while speaking with her media reps on the phone. Before long, boxes of candy, baskets of fruit, and an endless flow of complimentary theater tickets for our clients started arriving at our doorstep on a daily basis. My first thought was that the reps surely must be taking unfair advantage of Lynn's good nature by offering bribes for business! But careful scrutiny of her work revealed, to my astonishment, that her negotiations were resulting in media proposals for our clients that I couldn't have exceeded on my best day. I told her what a great job she was doing, and I didn't try to hide my amazement at her ability to get the job done effectively in her own way. She said six words: "You catch more bees with honey."

In hindsight, Lynn had taught her employer a most valuable lesson. As she explained it to me, people all want the same thing, regardless of which side of the table they happen to be sitting at. They want to be appreciated for what they do, they want to contribute to the success of the organization they work for, they want to do a good job, and they much prefer to work in an environment as free from stress as possible. As long as all that could be accomplished in a professional manner, with the desired results achieved, should it matter if the tone of the conversation was mild mannered versus emotionally demanding? Whether you're working with an ad agency, or handling these duties yourself, negotiating with a supplier, making a presentation to a customer, or coaching an employee, I learned this valuable lesson from my first employee: Bees respond so much more favorably to **A Taste Of Honey.** (Thank you, Ric Marlow and Bobby Scott!)

OI VAY

If you're not fluent in Yiddish, "Oi Vay Ish Mir" is an expression that is commonly accepted to mean "Oh Woe Is Me!" Most people, regardless of their ethnic background, are at least familiar with the shortened form of that expression, "Oi Vay!" When I tell you this story, I wish I could be there to see you throw your hands in the air, roll your eyes, and exclaim to the heavens, "Oi Vay!" Like all the stories presented in this book, this one is also true, though you may find it hard to believe!

Alan was ahead of his time by at least five years. As the owner of a major carpet distributorship, Alan's business involved acting as the middle-man between the various carpet manufacturers (mills) and the retail store owners who needed to buy their goods from the manufacturers. Since the mills were not (yet) in the business of selling directly to the retailers, the distributor enjoyed a position of power and importance in the negotiating process, from both sides. Looking five years into the future, as Alan did, the time came in the nationwide business consolidation movement that the middle-man got squeezed out of the process, as the mills looked to cut costs and thereby increase profits. Their easiest solution appeared obvious: eliminate the middle-man-distributor, and deal directly with the retail store owners. This shortsighted decision spawned the development of aggressive cooperative buying groups made up of retailers banding together to deal with the mills in a position of strength through negotiations based on volume purchasing. These buying groups gained even greater strength through larger numbers, and the mills eventually found themselves in an even worse position than before. But back to the story of Alan! He saw into the future, and realized the coming fate of

41

distributorships like his. He knew he needed to be something more than just a purchasing agent for his client retailers. Alan was wise enough to understand that the more he could do to help these retailers sell their product, the more product they would in turn need to buy from him. And what was the best way to help them sell more product? Advertising! So, Alan established what just might have been the first Advertising cooperative in the industry, putting together a group of 100 small independent retailers in the New York City metro who would make the first attempt at cooperating not only in their buying decisions, but in their Advertising, as well. Now, I must explain what made this as difficult as it was impressive. If you've ever tried to form a group to do anything, like getting together for dinner, or going to a ballgame, you know that it's virtually impossible to get everyone to agree on even the basics of where to go, what time to get there, and who pays the bill! Having worked with (too) many groups over the years, I can tell you that these little disagreements are magnified a hundred-fold in the business context. I challenge you to convince 100 small independent retail store owners to agree on even whether they should meet at all, let alone where to hold the meeting, what time, what day, and on and on, ad nauseam. After all, even though these merchants are banding together for their perceived common good, they are, in the final analysis, still competitors. It's not unusual that in some cases their retail stores were only blocks away from each other. But Alan had his vision, and the strength of character to get to first base, which was an organizational meeting for the 100 retailers he wanted in the group. Of course, it helped immeasurably that Alan wined and dined them at a posh New York restaurant, where the meeting took place after lunch.

I had been introduced to Alan by one of my clients, who owned a regional chain of carpet stores. Alan certainly could have had his pick of Madison Avenue ad agencies to make a presentation to his group. But he invited my client and this sixties hippie to fly to The Big Apple and address the group, recognizing that the key to their success would not be based on the prestige or size of the agency, but on their experience in the carpet industry. Smart man, that Alan! My role was to convince the group members that a group effort would enable them to do something that none of them could afford to do alone, advertise effectively to the masses. Perhaps in my next book, I'll give you a more formalized theoretical explanation of how that could be accomplished. But for now, I'll try to summarize the challenge much more briefly! Pretend, for the sake of argument, that you own a small carpet store in Manhattan (or a small any kind of store!). Your annual sales, which used to average around $1 million, have been dropping steadily each year for the past five, due to increasing competition and a tough economy. If someone were to ask your current annual sales, your pride would force you to respond, "about $2 million." In reality, fewer customers are walking into your store than ever before. The future looks pretty bleak. You decide you must take positive steps, so you start calling all the ad agencies you can find in the Yellow Pages, which in New York City is several thousand! The big ones won't talk to you because you're too small, and the small ones don't have a clue how to help you because they have no knowledge whatsoever of the carpet business, let alone the Advertising business! As you become more frantic about your financial future, your distributor calls to invite you to a presentation by an "Advertising expert from out of town," so you figure it couldn't hurt to attend, especially since Alan is buying lunch! After lunch, the speaker is introduced, and up to the podium strides this hippie with bushy full-face beard, curly mop of hair to the shoulders, dressed in jeans and sneakers (but at least he's wearing a tweed sport coat), and you think to yourself, "Oi Vay." In fact, you don't just think it, you say it aloud, along with the other 99 merchants in attendance. The hippie begins speaking, a bit nervous at first, then tells a joke or two in Yiddish, so he can't be all bad! Then you notice he's speaking very quietly, not at all what you expected from an expert brought in from out of town. And you decide it might make sense to *listen* to what he has to say, on the slight chance he might know something you don't know, despite his youth and appearance.

I had already decided that the key to getting agreement of any kind from this group was to arrive fully prepared, and to lay out a definitive Plan of Action rather than say "we could do this, or we could do that, but it's gonna cost you!" Believe me, I had done my home-work, and my briefcase was packed with not only spec commercials but printed proposals for each group member. "Here's the plan," I said. "I propose we run a major sales campaign on President's Day weekend, culminating in One Final Day on Monday, the holiday." Dead silence. Then, I played a sample TV commercial. A few mumbles. From the back of the room someone shouts, "OK, how much?" At this point, I knew I had them! The cost of my holiday weekend TV proposal was a mere $100,000, and full page ads in the New York Times only $50,000! Again, pretend you're that small store owner with annual sales below $1 million. $150,000 in media costs for a 3-day sale? That's 15% of your total annual gross sales! Now you understand why so few local merchants can afford to advertise in a city the size of New York, since the population is so large, and Advertising costs are based on the size of the audience you are reaching! But this is where the strength in numbers enters the equation. Divide that $150,000 cost by 100 stores, and each store only has to contribute $1,500. Even though $1,500 is still more money than you've ever spent on Advertising for a whole month, let alone 3 days, you decide it's worth a try after Alan steps up to the plate and offers to pick up a percentage of the Advertising tab, as well as the production costs for the commercials. Smart man, that Alan! I concluded the meeting by telling the merchants all money would be handled by Alan's office, and he would need their checks within a week, along with their signed approval of all the expenditures. They complied, and we were off and running.

There were many little problems to be overcome, as you might expect, but for the purposes of this chapter, everything went smoothly enough. Since we wouldn't be meeting with the merchants again until after the sale had concluded, I decided it would be extremely important to communicate all the details to them *before* the event, just to make sure they were fully prepared. Ten days before the holiday weekend, we overnighted the identical promotional package to each of the 100 store owners in the group. The package contained a written summary of what TV stations the commercials would air on, and the days and times they would air. Also included was a tear sheet of the newspaper ads that we had prepared, and a schedule of when they would run. Finally, I produced a 15-minute audio cassette presentation which detailed all the advance preparations each store should make for the sale. The cover page of the package proclaimed in big, block letters, LISTEN TO THIS TAPE BEFORE YOU DO ANYTHING ELSE! A week before the event, Lynn (see **Bees and Honey**) called all 100 owners by phone to make sure they had received and reviewed our presentation. President's Day Weekend came all too soon. This being the first major group effort I would be involved in, I was struck by the general feeling of helplessness! There I sat, hundreds of miles away from my clients, unable to see or hear my own commercials and ads, with no feedback of any kind. Confident as I may have been, I couldn't help but feel a sense of dread when I attended our second group lunch, this one a week after the holiday sales event.

I flew in to The City once again, and arrived at the restaurant with visions of 100 New Yorkers simultaneously "pulling an Irwin" on me! Much to my surprise, however, most of the merchants were very friendly, patting me on the back, smiling, and generally expressing their overall satisfaction with our first group effort. When I was called to the podium after lunch, I asked for comments from the participants about what they had experienced at their stores over the weekend, and I was shocked that not even one negative comment was offered. Then, out of the blue, one little old gentleman in the back of the room jumped up and screamed, "Oi vay! D'is vas the vorst d'ing I ever done! You t'ink you're some kinda hot shot, coming in here and taking my money? I did'n have even von customer in my store!" Gulp. There's nothing like one dissenter to destroy the camaraderie of the group. Frankly, I was dumbfounded. It seemed impossible to me that 99 stores were generally satisfied with their results, while only one experienced failure at my hands. I decided I needed more information, so I asked the gentleman, "Did you listen to the tape I sent you?" He answered, "No, I got no time for d'at...I'm a busy man." A few chuckles. I pressed on. "And no customers came into your store on Saturday, Sunday, or Monday? Not even one?" He just stood there looking at me with a very confused look on his face, and finally answered, "Saturday, Sunday and Monday vas a holiday, so ve vere closed!" Now it was my turn. I brought my hand to my forehead, rolled my eyes, and exclaimed to the heavens, "Oi Vay! Meeting adjourned!"

There are many lessons to be learned in this chapter, not the least of which is the potential benefits to be derived from group efforts. But perhaps the most important lesson is the necessity, as a merchant, to pay attention to the details! As buying groups and assorted franchise opportunities continue to dominate the current retail playing field, at some point you may just find yourself a member of such a group effort. When that time comes, please, *listen,* and pay close attention to the little things! That's **All I Ask of You.** (Thank you, Andrew Lloyd Weber!)

A SMALL FISH IN A BIG POND

I can't seem to remember where I met Eddie. Was it Dallas? Actually, it really doesn't matter, except it bothers me that I can't remember! Eddie faced a problem that is common to many business owners, which he raised as a question in one of my workshops. He owned a store in a small town on the fringes of the greater Boston market. It could just as well have been New York, Los Angeles, Detroit, Chicago, or any number of densely populated "major metro markets" and the problem would still be the same. How do you take your business to the "next plateau" of growth as a very small fish in a very large pond? Over the years, so many businesses just like Eddie's had found their local newspaper to be the perfect vehicle for addressing their local consumers. In the context of the stunning growth of the electronic media during the final quarter of the twentieth century, however, these towns were merely small cogs in a much larger wheel. As television became a superpower in the Advertising game, merchants in these towns were faced with the overwhelming challenge of competing with large, multi-store businesses which enjoyed the distinct advantage of being able to amortize their Advertising costs over a number of stores. In other words, if it costs $1 to advertise, and you own ten stores, you can spread that cost out as a thin dime per store. If you own only one store, that store must absorb and justify the entire $1 cost. It's probably important that you revisit the chapter, **Oi Vay**. We were discussing a group of 100 independently owned and operated businesses banding together in an experimental cooperative Advertising effort in New York City, thereby enabling the group to address the masses in a way that no single member of the group could ever afford to do alone. As you recall,

47

Advertising rates are based on population. The more people you reach, the more expensive the rates. And that's the problem with large cities...they have lots of people! It's one thing to invest $1,500 in a 3-day ad campaign as one of a group of 100, it's quite another to invest $150,000 in a solo effort! If you're lucky enough to be in the right place at the right time, and such a group opportunity presents itself, you almost have no choice but to take advantage of it. To ignore the potential financial benefits would be myopic. But what do you do if, like Eddie, there simply isn't any opportunity for such a cooperative venture? What if you have no choice but to go it alone? Are you destined to flounder forever in the local newspaper, never able to climb that next rung up the ladder of business growth unless you open a chain of stores that can afford to advertise?

What do I mean when I say "the fringes of the greater Boston major metro market"? Eddie's store was actually located in a small Massachusetts town many miles from Boston. If Eddie wanted to advertise on TV, his store was, by definition, within the geographic "coverage area" of Boston TV stations, based on the defined boundaries of the TV ADI (Area of Dominant Influence) map as structured by the gods of television station ownership under the guidelines of the FCC. Imagine, then, that you are Eddie. Your store has annual sales of about $1 million. You recognize that the only way to get to $2 million is to reach a larger audience. Your local newspaper isn't growing, it's shrinking, or at best remaining constant. You know you have to advertise on TV to reach the larger audience you've targeted. You invite the Boston TV stations to send an AE in to meet with you. If you're lucky, one might actually show up. Frankly, their reticence is to be expected, since they already know what you don't know, that no matter how you slice it, you'll be totally unprepared for the numbers you'll be presented. Like our New York example, you could easily spend $100,000 on a weekend to achieve the required "Reach" and "Frequency" levels to assure your success in the framework of Boston TV ad rates. Obviously, the numbers just don't make any sense. Even if you had $100,000 to invest, which you don't, and even if you were guaranteed your store would be mobbed for three days, it's probably a physical impossibility that even the best sales staff could be expected to write $1 million in business over three consecutive days just to justify your $100,000 *Advertising* investment! Think about it. $1 million in sales in three days? That's your gross sales volume for the entire year! So you say to the AE, "Look, I really want to try this, but I don't *need* to advertise to the millions of people living in Boston! They're not going to shop at my store anyway. I just want to reach this one, small corner of the market, within a twenty-mile radius of my store. Why can't I do that?"

The answer to that question is precisely why cable TV became such a power, so quickly. In major metro markets, the cost of Advertising on TV was prohibitive for small businesses, as detailed above. Let's face it, you can't just politely tell a TV broadcast signal to abruptly stop its predetermined journey through space and time! But you can tell a subterranean cable where to deliver its signal according to a predetermined coverage map of households at the other end of that cable. After all, it's your cable! TV broadcasters recognized the financial potential of dividing the major metro markets into well defined and manageable cogs in the much larger wheel, to continue the analogy first presented in the previous paragraph. Looking at this from the perspective of the broadcaster, imagine the potential of suddenly opening up the Advertising airwaves to the tens of thousands of businesses that couldn't afford to advertise on TV because of the too-broad scope of its coverage. A whole new market would be yours for the taking. Looking at this from the perspective of Eddie, imagine the potential of finally being able to carve out your market niche from a much smaller pie, at rates that were still based on population, of course, but greatly reduced by an equal reduction in the geographic (population) coverage area. Finally, Eddie could have his wish of reaching only the consumers within a twenty-mile radius of his store. This is what you call a win-win situation. At least, in design.

In the early years of cable TV, the reality was much different. For one thing, it would take many years before the cable systems could build up the required market penetration to deliver the audience levels its advertisers so desired. By market penetration, I mean the number of homes that paid for, and thus became wired to receive the cable signal. Early penetration numbers of 20% were common, which meant that only 20% of the homes in the defined region were wired to receive cable. Not a guarantee that the residents of those homes would actually be watching cable TV, just that they had the physical capability to do so. As I said, it took a long time to build up to acceptable penetration rates in the 80%+ range. The next problem was programming. As difficult as this may be to believe, given the current glut of cable programming, in the earlier days of cable there was a severe lack of programming. Indeed, many experts thought this would surely be the demise of the cable dream. But despite these and many other problems, cable did become the media monster it is today, a worthy Advertising vehicle for its local clients. And, as time progressed, cable TV extended its web beyond the major metro markets to the entire country, indeed the world. Today, distant and isolated regions of the country that can't effectively receive TV broadcast signals over the airwaves are probably wired for cable.

Let's get back to Eddie, standing there in my workshop waiting for an answer! "Eddie," I advised, "you need to try cable TV." Eddie was ready for that answer. "I already did, and it didn't work." I could easily digress again for many chapters, describing the reasons it didn't work, but for our purposes let me just say that cable TV is a different animal than network broadcast TV, and must be approached with different criteria. Given the very nature of the medium, it becomes even more essential that you pay particular attention to motivating the cable TV viewer with a strong offer (see **Give Them a Reason**). If you watch cable TV, you know that now more than ever, with the sheer number of stations and programs available to the viewer, the remote control has become a powerful tool in the hands of the consumer! So you better make your point, fast, and effectively. Not only that, but you simply can't rely on the cable Advertising sales department to structure an effective airtime schedule for you! By no means am I being cynical, but with the volume of 30-second blocks of time they have to sell, on the number of programs, over the number of stations they air on their system, their primary interest is to sell their inventory, which may not necessarily coincide with the audience you're attempting to reach. It's up to you (or your agent) to tell them what you want, when you want it. Eddie was willing to listen, and willing to give it another shot, bless his soul. His last comment to me was, "I live in Massachusetts, but I'm from Missouri, so I invite you to show me!"

As it turned out, Eddie's 20-mile target radius was a part of three different cable systems, each with coverage maps that overlapped his desired geography. So we structured a week-long schedule of airings on the appropriate programs in the appropriate systems. (Unlike network broadcast TV, it's extremely difficult, if not impossible, to achieve the necessary impact on one day of cable TV Advertising, which explains the week-long approach in favor of the one-day approach.) Just to cover our bases, Eddie also ran a small newspaper ad in his local paper to promote the event. Whereas the cost of Advertising a weekend event in the Boston major metro market could easily have exceeded $100,000, Eddie's three-system cable TV buy totaled $6,500 for the entire week, plus another $1,000 for newspaper. The sales figures he achieved amounted to 15 times his Advertising investment, which is well above the acceptable 10:1 ratio. Eddie was thrilled, as he should have been, and proceeded to tell others that "I told Jeff I was from Missouri and I wanted him to show me the results he said I could achieve. And do you know what? He did just that!" Happily, cable TV did the job for Eddie, for **The First Time Ever.** (Thank you, Roberta Flack!)

PROTECT YOUR RIGHTS

The first brother I met was George. He called my 800-# after seeing my ad in *Automotive News*, with the headline "Sell a month's quota of cars in 4 days!" One of my account executives spent time with George on the phone, and got him to the point where he was ready to license *The World's Greatest Car Sale* (see **Grab Their Attention**). Before George agreed to send in his check, he said, "I want to speak to the boss!" I would learn over the years that everyone wanted to speak with the boss, especially car dealers. No matter how knowledgeable and courteous the AE might be, apparently you're only as good as the head honcho. So, I took George's call, and was treated to a free education! "Look, Jeff, I'm gonna buy your sales event, at the price your guy quoted me, but I'll tell you something. You should be charging much more money for this! Not to me, of course, but if this works as well as I think it will, you're way under-priced." The three brothers owned three car dealerships in Philadelphia and South Jersey, having taken the reigns from their father, one of the first car dealers in the country! George was picked to be the guinea pig of the group and run the event at his Chevrolet dealership in Atlantic City. If all went well, the other brothers would likely run it at their dealerships. Even though Atlantic City is a good 90-minute drive from Philadelphia, it's still part of the Philadelphia major metro TV market, making television airtime prohibitive in cost. So, TV was out of the question. However, Atlantic City had the usual assortment of strong local radio stations, and a powerful regional newspaper. George sure knew how to use radio to his advantage. During the five days of radio Advertising for the sale, he owned the airwaves, as we say. I thought a spot-an-hour on the three top stations would have been more than adequate, but George bought four spots-an-hour on five stations! (See **I've Got the Fever**). In the newspaper, he ran two full-page ads, the first on the day before the sale, the second on the final day of the sale. After the event had concluded, I didn't hear from George for days. Finally, a week later, George called me, and I could hear two things in his voice: a smile, and exhaustion. "So, how did we do?" I asked. He answered, "Jeff, I wouldn't have believed it if I hadn't seen it with my own eyes! We had customers lined up 6-deep in the showroom. Listen, my brothers, Charlie and Frank, want to meet you. How soon can you fly down here?" The next morning, I was on my way to Atlantic City, another in a long list of gambling towns I would visit over the years, even though I never gambled! The only way into the city was on a "puddle-jumper," and the airport was an old military airfield, but there I was.

Charlie ran another dealership in Atlantic City. He decided not to run the event at his location, thinking it was just a little too aggressive in style. As the oldest brother, I guess he was the conservative one. Youngest brother Frank had driven down from his dealership in Philadelphia. He was ready to run the event at his place, and we hopped in the car to visit Frank's dealership. Impressive from the moment you approached, it was much more than just a massive car lot, loaded with about 1,000 vehicles. It also housed an indoor showroom bigger than most gymnasiums, boasting a 3-level display area, complete with a customer elevator. Had this place been a mall at one time? What I found most interesting was that Frank's dealership specialized not in new vehicles, like all the others I had worked with, but in used…sorry, pre-owned…Cadillacs and Lincolns. He also featured exotic cars, like Rolls Royce, Bentley, Lamborghini, Ferrari…you know, the cars you saw only in the movies. In Frank's case, a major promotional effort would be undertaken on Philadelphia network TV, radio, and full-page color ads in the prestigious Philadelphia Inquirer newspaper. It was all very exciting, and we looked forward to the event with eager anticipation. Frank handed me a check for advance payment, which he wasn't required to do. He also handed me another check, this one for the cost of my airplane ticket, which he also didn't have to do. We then drove back to Atlantic City, leaving enough time (I hoped) for me to catch my flight out at 8 o'clock that evening. Traffic was a nightmare the entire way back to Atlantic City, and after gathering my bag at the dealership, George's driver actually made a wrong turn on the way to the airport. He dropped me off at precisely 8 o'clock, with the departing comment that he would come back for me if there was any problem. I sprinted to the gate, only to see the plane taking off. No big deal, I thought to myself, I'll just catch the next flight. Yea, right. The next flight was the next day, at noon! I was ready to call George and ask to sleep on his couch for the night, when I saw a group of about fifteen people hanging around one of the gates. Never one to be shy, I asked what organization the group belonged to, and a rather rotund man explained that they had come in that morning on a privately chartered gambling shuttle. "Where did you fly in from," I asked. "Rochester, New York. Ever been there?" he asked in return. Maybe I *should* have gambled, for I sensed a bit of good luck! "Not only have I been there, I live there! In fact, I just missed my flight home a few minutes ago, so I'm stuck here for the night." I always knew Rochestarians were friendly, but I was now totally convinced of it, as he asked, "Why don't you fly home with us? We've got an extra seat or two on the plane." I smiled, dug out my wallet (which was empty of any green stuff), and was shocked when he said, "Naw, put that away. Just get on the plane with me, no one will know the difference." A true gentleman if I ever met one. Just so you won't think I'm a "taker" and not also a "giver," I learned on the flight home that he had been shopping for a new car for weeks, unable to find a deal he was comfortable with. I wrote down Jay's phone number (see **Grab Their Attention**), and told the gentleman to call Jay and use my name. About a week later, he actually called me at my office to tell me Jay had sold him a car for thousands of dollars less than the best deal he had been quoted anywhere else. I felt better.

I won't bore you with a text book approach to audience demographics, because common sense (so often lacking in Advertising) tells you that the people who buy and drive Cadillacs and Lincolns are typically "older," which means 55 years of age and up. As a result, you won't be surprised to discover that Advertising on radio stations in those days referred to as "Easy Listening" was key to the successful outcome of Frank's sales event. I've described the event previously in **Grab Their Attention**, and you may wish to revisit that section to refresh your memory. Suffice it to say that *The World's Greatest Car Sale* is a very assertive and strong promotion, not only in the words it uses, but also in the production style it employs. When you hear it on the air, it really sounds like a mini-Star Wars movie, complete with modernistic sound effects of swooshing comets and thunderous explosions of energy. Literally the day before Frank's event was scheduled to hit the airwaves, something happened that was a first for me, and I hoped the last. Out of the five radio stations on which we had purchased airtime, three were Easy Listening in format, and all three called to inform me that the spots I had produced couldn't be aired on their stations. This was my introduction to Philadelphia radio! I asked why not, and was told the same thing by all three General Managers. "While we appreciate your business, we are, after all, in the business of satisfying our listeners. Frankly, we find this material to be offensive in its presentation style, much too aggressive for our listeners." To say I was stunned would be the understatement of the decade. But wait, there was more! "Actually, this is quite common for us, and we'll gladly accommodate you by re-recording your commercials with one of our on-staff announcers, without all the loud music and noise. That way, your commercials will sound just like all the other commercials on our station, and everyone will be happy. Oh, by the way, I'm afraid we'll have to leave out the part in your script about roller skating home and banging your head against a brick wall...our listeners wouldn't stand for that!" I was way beyond stunned, now, I was mad! "I'll call you back in 15 minutes," was all I could muster as a response.

I got on the horn with Frank and told him what had just happened. I knew darn well that giving in to their demand would doom this major (and expensive) promotional effort to certain failure. This wasn't just my pride talking. It was the conviction that the success of my promotion was built upon a foundation of many variables, not the least of which were the words, the music, and the impressive array of sound effects, not to mention the dramatic voice-over delivered by yours truly. These very elements had made *The World's Greatest Car Sale* the attention grabber that it was! Frank was pretty upset, this being the day before the sale, and considering all the money he had invested I was surprised he took it as well as he did. "Do what you have to do, Jeff," was all he could think to say. After we disconnected, I thought to myself that's just what I'll do…what I have to do. Perhaps someone else would have said "Why should I care, it's not my money?" But I did care!

I called each of the three GM's back in order, saying the same to each. "The spots I shipped to you will air as produced, or they won't air at all. They are copyrighted productions, and I own the copyright. Changing them without my written authorization is a violation of federal copyright law, and I will pursue legal remedies if you violate my rights." That got 'em…or so I thought! Each responded with the same comment. "In that case, since we will not air these commercials in their present form, we will not air anything." That got me…or so they thought! I took a deep breath and answered, "OK, no problem. Cancel the schedules." They protested, "You can't cancel a schedule the day before it airs!" "I just did," I replied. I may not have been a gambler, and I may never have played cards, but I had just taken my best shot at keeping a straight Poker face. To my delight, they folded. The spots ran as ordered, as produced. And, Frank's dealership experienced the most successful sales event in their history, which is saying something, since it was founded in the second decade of the twentieth century!

Whatever you do, don't give away your rights! After all, it's your money we're talking about. You'll encounter many such situations in your own business activities. I urge you to know your rights, and protect them, **Body and Soul.** (Thank you, John Green!)

HONOR THE RIGHTS OF OTHERS

Truth is indeed stranger than fiction. When you read this story, you're bound to think I'm making it up just for the sake of writing a chapter. But I assure you this is exactly as it happened. Lynn buzzed me on the intercom one morning to tell me I had a call on hold from a car dealer named Rick. "He doesn't sound too happy," Lynn warned. Just between you and me, I hate taking calls from disgruntled people, especially first thing in the morning. It has a way of upsetting your whole day. I always try to remind myself that for every hundred people you deal with, one complaint isn't so bad in the scope of things. Bracing myself for the worst, I picked up and said hi to Rick. Much to my surprise, he didn't sound all that angry after all, just disappointed. "You know, I ran one of your ads last week in the newspaper, and it didn't work at all. But I thought I'd give you another shot and try the whole campaign, you know, with the TV and radio this time. Maybe even let you handle the whole ball of wax for me." *OK, this doesn't sound so bad,* I thought to myself. I asked Rick the name of his dealership and what city he was in. He paused for a moment, then gave me the information I had asked him for. Although I had over 200 car dealerships as clients at this point in time, my memory never failed me when it came to names and cities. But I was stumped. "Rick, I'm a little embarrassed to say this, but I don't have any recollection of you licensing any of my work." His response floored me. "Oh, I didn't actually license anything, but I did run one of your ads." I pressed on. "Rick, how did you do that?" Once again, his answer knocked me for a loop. "Well, to be honest with you, I saw your ad in *Automotive News*, and I liked it, so I had my newspaper rep blow it up and put my logo on it." My heartbeat accelerated rapidly as I asked,

"Rick, did you happen to notice the little 'c' in a circle, along with my name and the date?" He answered, "Oh, yeah, I had my rep erase it so it wouldn't ruin the looks of the ad." By now, my blood was bubbling, as they say. As diplomatically as I could, I said "Rick, what you removed was a legal copyright notice, identifying me as the owner of that ad. Do you realize that what you did was not only unethical, but illegal?" His response put me down for the count! "Heck, I didn't think you'd mind, especially since I'm calling you now to ask about buying the whole campaign, even though it didn't work the first time!" I needed time to think. In situations like this, when you feel like you're going to start screaming obscenities, it's best to cool down before you say anything you'll regret. "Rick, I'll call you back later today."

As I calmed myself, the whole picture suddenly came into focus. The final missing piece in a confusing puzzle had been provided. Only a week earlier, one of my AE's had been on the verge of wrapping up a contract with another car dealership in the same city that Rick had just called from. It was to be the start of a very nice and profitable working relationship that would have netted the agency about $40,000-a-year in commissions. After weeks of negotiating, it seemed like the deal was in the bag, and we eagerly awaited a signed agreement from our new client. Without explanation, the contract never arrived. Worried it had been lost in the mail, the AE called the dealer and was reprimanded in the following way: "You know, I thought I could trust you guys, but I guess that was wishful thinking on my part. I've decided to work with a local agency." *Click*. Numerous phone calls from the AE went unanswered, and we just chalked it up to a situation out of our control. Now, sitting at my desk recounting the phone conversation I had just had with Rick, it came into focus all too clearly. The newspaper ad Rick had *borrowed* without permission was taken from the very same campaign the other dealer was ready to license. After all our written and verbal assurances that he would receive market exclusivity, meaning that no other dealer in his market would be able to use this campaign, you can only imagine his level of distrust when he opened his local newspaper and saw another dealer running the ad. Naturally, he blamed us, thinking we were attempting to scam him, a practice all too common to the industry.

I called my attorney. Then I called Rick. I explained to him what had happened as a result of his actions, and I offered him the opportunity to make amends. I thought this was more than fair under the circumstances. "One, you can license the campaign for the year at a cost of $40,000. Two, you can call the other dealer and tell him what happened and why. If he decides to follow through on his working relationship with us after learning we weren't at fault, you'll be off the hook without a penny out-of-pocket. Three, we can initiate legal action against you." I then suggested that Rick speak with his attorney before making his decision, since a copyright infringement action under these circumstances would be a slam-dunk, and would end up costing him more money than any of the other options I had suggested. Rick decided not to take any time to calm himself before answering, "Sue me!" *Click.* That day, my attorney visited the library, obtaining a copy of the newspaper from the city in question on the day Rick's ad would have run. Sure enough, there it was. He made a copy of the offending ad. Next, he called the newspaper and spoke with the rep who was said to have blown up the ad and removed the copyright notice. He told a different story. When he received the ad from Rick, the notice had already been removed, and he had no way of knowing it was copyrighted material. He provided an affidavit. Finally, my attorney contacted the other dealer, requesting (and receiving) an affidavit attesting to his cancellation of our proposed working agreement based on seeing Rick's ad in the newspaper. Within two weeks, we were awarded a summary judgment for willful violation of copyright, which Rick was obligated to pay.

Over the years, I learned the hard way that the Advertising game is unscrupulous. I can't tell you how many times businesses, indeed other ad agencies, *borrowed* from me without my knowledge, let alone my permission. Don't misunderstand, borrowing ideas is commonplace and accepted. Nobody owns the rights to a name, like *Holiday Sale,* or *Super Sale.* But when you use someone else's graphic representation (artwork) or written word (script) in violation of their legally filed copyright notice, that's a definite no-no. In fact, I came to find out quite by accident that my ads were being included in several "clip services" without my permission. A "clip service" spends its time in the library going through newspaper ads from hundreds of cities each week. They pick out the best ads and compile a weekly or monthly catalog of those ads which they sell to their subscribers all across the country, promoting their service as a way for local businesses and ad agencies to see the best of the best in exchange for a minimal monthly subscription fee. Eventually, "clip services" expanded into TV and radio, providing their subscribers with video and audio ad samples copied from the public airways. They get around the copyright issue by claiming they aren't actually selling the ads, but merely providing samples of what other advertisers are doing as an informational service for their subscribers. Would you like to know how I came to find out I was being "honored" as a regular contributor to their service? You guessed it. I received a direct mail piece from them, followed by a phone call from a telemarketer, offering to sell me my own ads as part of their monthly service! I don't mind admitting to you that I strongly object to others making money off my ideas without seeing a penny myself. That's not greed speaking, it's pride in my work, and the belief in a code of ethics in business which is sadly lacking. Something is definitely very wrong when you reach the unpleasant realization that you could actually make more money in the courts *protecting* your work than in the marketplace *selling* your work! My advice to you? Don't play with fire. You'll get burned. Walk a mile in someone else's shoes, if you will. Your sense of fair play is but a part of **All The Things You Are.** (Thank you, Jerome Kern!)

CHOOSE YOUR BED MATES CAREFULLY

Aha! I caught you, sneaking to this chapter directly from the Table of Contents without reading previous chapters in the order intended! Why did you do it? You did it because sex sells. As long as you're here, you're welcome to read on, but I must first warn you, *It ain't what you're thinkin'!* In the Advertising game, an agency and its client are said to "get into bed" with one another, as the closeness of the relationship rivals only marriage. If you've selected the right agency, you'll soon regard your agent as a good bed mate. If you've selected the wrong bed mate, it will be painfully obvious to both of you tomorrow morning! Understand, you certainly aren't required to use the services of an ad agent. But if you're going to use one, find the one you think you're willing to get into bed with, and then give him enough rope. You'll soon learn whether your agent will hang himself with that rope (figuratively, of course), or take up the slack and keep pulling. Agencies are like people. Actually, they *are* people! And they all have their own personalities and specialties. My own particular forte has always been *Retail Advertising.* Many agencies won't touch retail accounts. They're just not equipped. Even within the limited retail specialty, I focused even further on *big ticket* retail accounts, like car dealers, home furnishings and appliance stores, floor covering stores, and the like. You'll run into agents who will tell you they "do it all." Don't believe them. It can't be done. Would you visit an eye doctor to remove a bunion from your foot? Agencies also specialize by media. Some are more adept in the print media, while others conquer the airwaves. You'll need to talk with several, listen carefully, and avoid getting into bed with the wrong partner. Nothing is worse than waking up the morning-after to the realization you've chosen the wrong bed mate. (At least, so I've been told!) Simply put, we all make mistakes. Not all clients (or agents) are nice people, and not all agency/client relationships are good or productive. The one I'm about to describe was a nightmare, not only for me, but also for the client, I'm sure. In short, we were terrible bed mates! Luckily, our marriage didn't suffer too long. I describe the relationship here in the positive context of making the point of the chapter for your benefit.

Remember meeting Herb, in **Concentrate Your Efforts?** As I mentioned, Herb was always recommending me to someone! In this case, based upon Herb's kind words, I was hired by a respected furniture manufacturer to plan and produce a special promotional event for retail stores that would hopefully participate in the manufacturer's introduction of a new product line in cities across the United States and Canada. In conjunction with the announcement and demonstration of that event, I was invited to present a series of Advertising workshops in the manufacturer's display showroom at the semi-annual furniture market in North Carolina. Like other buying markets in other cities, this one was housed in a seemingly endless maze of home furnishing showrooms in a complex of buildings that seemed to blanket a dozen city blocks. This is where the furniture manufacturers display their wares for furniture retailers, who attend specifically to purchase their goods for the coming year, hoping that we, the consumers, will buy what they've selected to sell to us. Our plan was that by combining an educational workshop with the special event introduction/demonstration, we would achieve better participation among the furniture retailers, which is precisely what happened. But something else happened, which I'll now tell you about.

Jane attended one of my Advertising workshops. The manufacturer that hired me had warned me in advance about what ended up actually happening. "If a woman named Jane attends your workshop, be careful. She's tough! She'll probably invite you to meet her husband, John, who handles the Advertising for their store. Whatever you do, don't take them on as an account. They'll chew you up and spit you out without another thought. And you wouldn't be the first." Perhaps like you, tell me not to do something and it makes me want to do it all the more, just to prove I can handle anything you don't think I can! Sure enough, Jane made an appearance at the workshop, and she was indeed tough! Surprise of surprises, she invited me to meet her husband, John, to discuss how I might be able to help them grow their already well established business, and the trap was set. The trap was then sprung when I was appointed ad agency of record for their large home furnishings store. Naturally, Jane and John checked out all my references before hiring me, and we reached what seemed an equitable agreement on how to tackle the problem at hand. I should tell you that my presentation to them was not unlike any others I've described in this book. I listened closely to all their ideas, problems, and goals, whereupon I detailed exactly how I would handle their account. Everyone signed on the dotted line, and we seemed to be off to the races, as they say. I didn't even give a moment's thought to the warning I had received from the manufacturer. When I later proudly told him about the working agreement I had just inked with Jane and John, he just shook his head slowly, and said, "Don't say I didn't warn you." If only I had listened!

Over the next several weeks, I formulated all my plans for their store, excited at the prospect of helping this organization reach the next plateau of business development. Interestingly enough, all my conversations were now with John. Jane's responsibility was running the store, while John's was the Advertising. Then the problem came into focus, all too clearly. John was what you might call a "control freak." No matter what I presented, it was diametrically opposed to John's personal experience. My media mix was "wrong," my promotional concepts were "wrong," I was "wrong," and the world was "wrong." As a result, John ended up modifying everything I proposed to the point where it became merely a reflection of the way he'd been doing things for years. He agonizingly rewrote my ad copy word by word, until it was virtually a carbon copy of what he himself had been writing before hiring me. He restructured my promotions until they were no different from his own that hadn't worked before, which was why I'd been brought on board in the first place. He torpedoed my media buys until he was comfortable they resembled what he was used to doing. Listen, I loved to argue with most of my clients, because it was always a healthy discussion of what's best for accomplishing the goals we had agreed on reaching. But in this case, the arguments were not only one-sided, they were brutal and demeaning. It didn't take long before John and I dreaded even speaking to each other over the phone. Finally, I lamented to John "I have no idea why you hired me! You don't listen to a thing I say, and you end up doing what you want anyway, so why pay me? Just do it all yourself. Life's too short for this nonsense."

As if to prove who was boss, John went on the air heavily that first month with hearty TV and radio expenditures, plus full page newspaper ads to support the electronic media. Since his store was located in a major media market, this was no inexpensive undertaking! Literally within hours of the campaign hitting the airwaves, John called me by phone, and I knew that this client wasn't "pulling an Irwin" on me. "Your ads are bringing in the wrong kind of customers." Unsure how to respond, I merely asked, "What do you mean, the wrong kind of customers?" John answered, "These are not our customers. These people can't afford to buy here. They're just wasting our time. I don't want them in my store. My sales people have more important things to do than waste their time on people that don't belong here in the first place." I was flabbergasted. "John, I wasn't aware *any* customer could be considered the *wrong kind* of customer. The way I see it, a customer is a person who has responded to your invitation to shop in your store, and is a potential buyer. How can you say that *any* customer is a waste of your time?" John proceeded to deliver a stinging answer to my question by all too specifically describing the kind of people he wanted in his store, and the kind he didn't. It wasn't pleasant. It wasn't even nice. There was nothing I could say other than remind John that *my* ads couldn't be blamed for his perceived problem, because they weren't my ads, after all, but his ads, written in his own hand. My ads could be found lining his garbage can! And if the people showing up in his store weren't *affluent* enough for his tastes, it couldn't be blamed on *my* media demographics, which never made it any farther than John's wastebasket. I could continue for pages, but I think you get the idea. We were terrible bed mates, and our ill-advised marriage resulted in a not-quickly-enough annulment.

You may not need or want to hire an ad agency. You may be perfectly capable of doing it all yourself, and that's fine. But if you're going to hire an agent to handle your Advertising for you, find the best one you can, with the specialty that most closely meets your needs, then jump into bed! If you don't choose wisely, you do yourself a great disservice, to say nothing of the agent. In my case, given the benefit of many years since the *Ambush at the Manufacturer's Coral,* the entire scenario I described remains nothing more than **A Foggy Day**. (Thanks again, George Gershwin!)

GIVE THEM A REASON

Terry was a disembodied voice over the telephone. He introduced himself as an installer for a small carpet store somewhere in smaller-town New Mexico, making sure I understood that he was going to take advantage of the opportunity recently presented to him of buying out the store's owner. Terry explained that he had read one of my feature articles about effective Advertising, which had recently been published in a national trade magazine. I may be gullible, but the typical carpet installer wasn't in the habit of reading trade magazines in favor of another kind of magazine, if you know what I mean! Terry confided that business was so slow where he worked, he had nothing better to do than read all the magazines in the store! OK, I'll buy that. Never having owned his own store, Terry asked all variety of questions, not all of them related to Advertising! It was my dime(s) paying for the toll-free-800-call, after all, but I was enjoying the conversation. So, we talked for the better part of an hour. I invited Terry to "keep in touch" and let me know how his plans developed. Over the next two years, I would hear from Terry every 6 months or so. The store he was working for was deteriorating rapidly, and Terry was preparing for his once-in-a-lifetime chance at ownership. He astutely recognized that the biggest problem at this store was the lack of Advertising. Not the lack of good Advertising, but the lack of any! "Jeff," he complained, "we're being eaten alive by the competition." After that call, I didn't hear from Terry for over a year, and I assumed that he had either left that store for greener (browner?) pastures, or the store had finally gone the way of so many small retailers, the dreaded GOB (Going Out of Business) Sale. Strange as it may sound, a GOB Sale is *always* a great sale! Some would say the reason is that people are akin to vultures. Personally, I'm not quite that cynical. I just think everybody loves a bargain, and a GOB can be a BHP (Bargain Hunter's Paradise). In many cases, the GOB Sale is actually the store's first attempt at Advertising! If only…well, at this point, it's too late. Or is it? Once hooked on the excitement and virtually guaranteed results of a GOB Sale, a number of business owners have been known to run them again…and again…and again. Unfortunately (for them), that's frowned upon by the Attorneys General in any state in the nation, and can result in a heavy fine and/or imprisonment for the perpetrator, depending on the severity of the infraction!

I was conducting another one of my Advertising workshops, this one in Reno, NV, for the benefit of a regional floor covering franchiser and it's franchisees. Now that I think about it, so many of the Advertising workshops and seminars I've conducted seem to have been held in gambling towns, like Las Vegas, or Reno. I guess that's appropriate, since most business owners equate Advertising with gambling…success is a shot-in-the-dark! If they only knew, Advertising is just the opposite! It's as close to guaranteed results as you can hope for, if done properly. In spite of all the time I've spent in gambling towns, I've never "invested" one cent in the slots, on the tables, or in any other kind of gamble. I just don't believe in it, nor do I enjoy it, but I recognize that many people relish the thrill of anticipation. I do have a vice or two, but drinking alcohol isn't one of them, either, so I couldn't even waste time at the bar before delivering my workshop three hours later! Bored, I parked myself on a couch in the hotel lobby and engaged in my favorite hobby, people-watching. An hour or so later, my eyes were about to close when I heard this familiar Southwestern drawl. "Haaaahhh, Jeff, Aahhm Terry!" It seems Terry had been invited to attend my workshop by the franchiser, even though Terry wasn't yet a franchisee. But he was close to becoming one! Yes, he had persisted and finally bought out the store's owner. Now an owner himself, he was considering purchasing a franchise, but wanted to ask my opinion. I told him I thought this franchise would be good for him, but that the ultimate success of his new operation would be determined, in my humble opinion, by the effectiveness of his Advertising. He readily agreed, and said he was looking forward to my workshop, now only minutes from beginning!

Whenever I conduct an Advertising workshop, I like to begin by asking a few general questions of the participants. My first question is usually "How many of you *don't* advertise?" Invariably, several brave souls will resolutely raise their hands with pride, as if Advertising is a mortal and moral sin and its avoidance guarantees entrance through the Pearly Gates! "Why don't you advertise?" I'll ask, and they'll answer in unison, "We don't have to! People know where to find us, and we have more business than we can handle without having to advertise." I glanced over at Terry, who was seated in the front row, and he chuckled and winked in understanding. I'm always tempted to challenge that pat answer by asking, "why, then, are you attending this workshop?" But that would be impolite. So I invite them to participate, nonetheless, and to feel free to offer their opinions at the close of the session. The next question I ask of the remaining majority is *"Why* do you advertise?" I ask the participants to write their answers down and pass them to the front, whereupon I read them aloud. The answers are *always* the same, regardless of geography, time of year, their industry, or the size of their business:

> We know we should advertise, so we do
>
> We want to keep our name out there in front of the public
>
> We want to sell our merchandise
>
> My brother-in-law is in the ad business (and needs a job), so he does our advertising for us
>
> We buy ads in the Church newspaper and write them off as charitable donations

Next, I'll ask, "*What* do you say in your ads?" Again, I'll ask for written answers to read aloud, and they rarely vary:

We've been in business for *xyz* years
We offer great products with great service
We're open convenient hours
Our prices are the best around

Now, it's not my intention to deliver an entire workshop here in this chapter! However, from the perspective of addressing Terry's needs, I can tell you that the most important thing you can do in your Advertising is give consumers a reason to shop at your store. In fact, not just a reason to shop, but a reason to shop today, right now! Take a look at the offered reasons to shop, introduced above, and imagine your own response, as a consumer!

We've been in business for *xyz* years: "So what!"

We offer great products with great service: "So does everyone else!"

We're open convenient hours: "You should be!"

Our prices are the best around: "Prove it!"

This is as good a time as any to introduce you to **Resnick's** *Advertising* **Truth #1: The American Consumer Has Been Trained to Shop for a Bargain!** The key word here is "trained." Like it or not, as consumers, we have all been trained in particular behavior patterns by years of exposure to Advertising strategies designed by devious people like me. If you need proof, just leaf through the ads in this Sunday's newspaper. Better yet, flip on your TV or radio. Count the ads that scream out, "Up to 50% Off!" In densely populated metropolitan areas, it has even become difficult to remember what retailer is running what ad, their ads are so similar! Unfortunately, most business owners don't understand the difference between the *Perception* and the *Reality* of **Truth #1.** The following true story (honest, it's *really* true!) perfectly illustrates this important but misunderstood difference. A client of mine, a carpet store owner (this *is* a workshop for carpet store owners, remember?), once confided a deep, dark secret that he'd withheld even from his $100-an-hour therapist! It seems that the daughter of his wife's best friend was getting married. As a genuine gesture of friendship, he called his wife's best friend, and offered to install new carpeting in the newlyweds' new home...at his cost! An appointment was scheduled to pick out the carpet after the wedding. The wedding came and went. The appointment was missed. Weeks later, the merchant and his wife received an invitation to attend the housewarming for the newlyweds' new home. No sooner did they step through the front door than they noticed the plush new carpeting throughout. The bride's mother must have seen the merchant's jaw drop in surprise, because she ushered him into the kitchen and confessed, "I'm so embarrassed! I know you wanted to take care of the kids, but they saw an ad for a half-price sale at this other carpet store, and they just couldn't pass up such a great deal. I hope you understand." The merchant was effusive in his attempt to smooth over the situation. After all, it's not worth ruining a friendship over. Upon returning to the living room to rejoin the party, he couldn't help but recognize the new carpet as one that he stocked in his own store. He approached the groom, smiled conspiratorially, and whispered, "What'd you pay for the carpet, Henry?" Proud of his newly realized business acumen, Henry replied, "Oh, we just got an unbelievable deal! This carpet usually sells for $40-a-yard, but they were having this incredible half-price sale, so we got it for just 20 bucks-a-yard! I even got them to throw in the pad and the installation for free!" The merchant nodded blankly, too shocked to respond that he sold this very carpet in his store, day-in and day-out, for $18-a-yard, including a better grade of pad, as well as lifetime-guaranteed installation.

Henry *perceived* that he got a great deal on his carpeting, so he was happy. The half-price retailer knew the *reality* of the sale, so he was happy. The proverbial bottom line is that both parties were happy! Although the consumer will always wonder if he might have done better elsewhere, and the retailer will always wonder if he could have got another dollar-a-yard for his carpet, they shake hands and thank the carpet gods that they each got (made) such a great deal. And that's the very nature of retail. But there was another *reality* at work here! Our merchant friend knew that his everyday price ($18) was lower than the "sale" price ($20) down the street, where they were screaming "50% Off!" Unfortunately, he never even got the chance to tell the consumer his *reality*, because the consumer *perceived* a bargain elsewhere. The true irony, in this case, is that our merchant had generously offered to sell the carpet at his cost to the bride and groom, as a gesture of friendship to the bride's parents! Incidentally, actual dealer cost on this carpet, including freight, was $6-a-yard, plus $5-a-yard for the pad and installation, totaling $11-a-yard. The total purchase of the required 75 yards of carpet, at "half-price," amounted to $1500. The total purchase at our merchant's everyday, "not on sale" price, would have been $1350 (with a better pad, at that). Regrettably for the bride and groom, the total purchase at our merchant's cost would have been $825. The carpet was exactly the same carpet, regardless of which store was selling it. The determining factor in this consumer's purchase had little or nothing to do with the carpet, and more to do with the successful *Advertising* presentation used by the "half-price" retailer. Successful, because he made the sale. And he could only make the sale by first getting the consumer into his store, which, if you remember, is the very purpose of Advertising! The real issue here is how one merchant's "half-price" can actually be more than another merchant's "regular price." Hmm . . .that's another workshop!

I'm now going to show you (a recreation of) an actual newspaper advertisement (minus the dealer's name) that actually ran every week for 52 weeks, with no changes. Before you look at it, please understand that I am by no means recommending that you run an ad like this! In truth, the ad was mailed to me by a competing merchant as an example of what he was up against in his marketplace. There are certainly many things you could say about this ad and about the store owner who produced it and used it. If nothing else, this merchant had learned how to play the game of Advertising, and had learned well. You must admit, he gives not one, but several reasons to shop at his store, today, right now. Admittedly, he takes this lesson to the absolute limits of commercial acceptability!

At the conclusion of the workshop, Terry congratulated me on the presentation, indicating that he had indeed learned what he came to learn. I've addressed a number of topics in this chapter, but all revolve around the very premise of giving consumers a reason to shop at your place of business, today, right now. You must use your own best judgment in deciding how far to take the lesson! Whether you agree or not, some would readily say **Anything Goes**. (Thanks again, Cole Porter!)

I'VE GOT THE FEVER

There was a time when the waterbed industry enjoyed a boom. I guess it was just a sign of the times, as they say, and if you were "Johnny on the spot," you could make a killing selling waterbeds. When you get right down to it, how strange is it that we would figure out a way to install a small lake in our bedrooms, not to swim in, not to sail on, not to ice skate on, not to fish in, but to sleep on? I remember my first waterbed, before they had heaters. It felt like you were sleeping on a morgue gurney, cold and clammy. Smelled just as bad, too. To be honest, once I bought my first waterbed heater, it was great! In the summer, when it was too hot to sleep, you could turn the heater off and let your bed cool you down. In the winter, when it was too cold to sleep, you could turn the heater on to warm you up, without having to heat the entire house. I can remember waking up on those cold Western New York mornings. You could see your breath (and you were still in the house), but you were nice and toasty in your heated waterbed. Like scores of other Americans, we even bought waterbeds for our kids! Then came all the other waterbed related products, like special fitted sheets and pillowcases, down comforters, headboards with built-in everything, fill and drain kits, water treatment chemicals (to prevent mold and odor), even waveless waterbed mattresses to keep your bed from sloshing from side to side every time you...uhmm...turned over. There were only two problems, both of which were pretty major! One, no upper floor apartments would allow waterbeds, afraid that the weight of the water would bring the bed crashing through the floor to the apartment below. Two, if you sprung a leak, you ran the risk of drowning in your own bed! Just picture that obituary.

Dick called me one day, introducing himself as the owner of a chain of waterbed stores. He admitted that he was particularly impressed with the way I had been using TV for my clients, not merely as an image builder, the way TV had been used for years, but as a powerful promotional vehicle, much like the way radio was being used by others. I had earned a pretty impressive track record by developing a format for my clients' TV ads that "counted down" the promotional events on a daily basis. What made this unusual was not the concept of counting down, which had been utilized in radio ads for years, but using this concept in TV spots, which heretofore had been pretty generic and institutional, a polite way of saying *unexciting*. For example, the day before the event started we would air a TV spot that said, "Sale starts tomorrow, quantities limited so shop early for best selection!" On the evening of that first day, we would switch to the second TV spot in the series, "Hurry, only 2 days left. When it's gone, it's gone!" On the evening of the second day, we would switch spots again to the third in the series, "Listen, turkey, it's over tomorrow, so get your rear-end in here before you miss out on the most unbelievable savings opportunity you've ever seen!" All of this would be supported with radio ads utilizing the same countdown approach, right through the final day of the sale. "You still have time, but this sale will be history at midnight tonight! So what are you waiting for?" In fact, now that I think about it, we took radio to the next step, too, counting down not just by days, but by hours. It wasn't unusual for us to air several different radio ads on any given day, taking the listener on a well conceived timed journey through the days and hours of our event. Eventually, the challenge became not how to end the event, but how to prolong it! "This sale was supposed to end today. For all of you who just couldn't fight the crowds, and left before a sales agent could help you, please accept our apology. For you, we've decided to extend this sale for one more day, tomorrow!" Coupled with a high impact media philosophy, concentrated over a short period of time (see **Concentrate Your Efforts**), this approach proved extremely successful for many years. I have no intention of giving you the standard text book definitions of media terms such as "Reach" and "Frequency," but I will dig down below the surface and try to explain to you how and why it all worked the way it did. I actually gave this approach a name, which caught on in the industry. I called it "Psychographic Persuasion."

For the moment, put yourself in the place of the typical consumer, an exercise I often undertook when designing my ad campaigns. Your clock radio awakens you at 6 am, and you're treated to a radio commercial announcing Dick's waterbed sale. You throw on your sweats and head out for your morning jog or, in my case, brisk walk, complete with Walkman radio and headphones to keep you company. You're treated to another commercial for the sale that starts tomorrow at Dick's waterbeds. You return home, shower, dress, and peruse the daily paper over a cup of coffee at the kitchen table (which, of course, you bought at Irwin's dinettes), only to see a full-page ad announcing the spectacular 3-day half-price sale that starts tomorrow at Dick's waterbeds. You catch a few minutes of the Today Show (or Good Morning America, or CNN, or CBS This Morning) before leaving for the office, and you notice a TV commercial for the incredible, mind-blowing, spectacular, 3-day, half-price, store-wide sale at Dick's waterbeds that starts tomorrow. You get in your car for your morning commute and turn on your favorite radio station. You guessed it. You arrive at the office, jump on the elevator for the ride up to the fourth floor and…yep, there it is again. You turn on the noon news on TV as you devour your lunch at your desk…this is getting a bit much. It continues on the drive home, then watching the evening news on TV, even during Wheel of Fortune! Is nothing sacred? You just can't escape it, no matter which channel you turn to. By the end of the day, you find yourself thinking, "Gee, something big must be happening over at Dick's waterbeds. Maybe we should check it out. Honey, have you thought about a waterbed?" The next day, you pile the kids into the car and drive over to Dick's waterbeds, just to see if anything is really going on. You can't find a space to park, since their lot is full, so you park two blocks away, along with hundreds of other people who are walking from their cars to Dick's store. You enter the store to see people flocking the aisles, salesmen doing their best to keep up with the traffic in the showroom. You can't help but notice that there's actually a line of people at the cash register waving their checkbooks and credit cards, impatiently waiting to pay for their new waterbeds. And you think to yourself, "Gee, maybe we better buy our waterbed right now before they're all gone!" That, ladies and gentlemen, is "Psychographic Persuasion," culminating in a severe case of impulse buying fever! This disease is any business owner's dream. Once you've experienced it, you'll never want to settle for anything less. And what of Dick's waterbeds? As you might expect, **It's The Talk of the Town.** (Thank you, Jerry Livingston!)

DOT COM GOES DOT BUST

The Internet was new to me, just as it was to everyone. Before I had even learned enough about it to set up my own web page, I received a call from a business owner inviting me to participate in a "can't miss" Internet company. The "Deal" (I hate that word) promised stock options, a healthy consulting fee, and the opportunity to put my skills to work once again in the national arena. It sounded interesting, so I attended a meeting with the CEO. Gary was a real winner, without question the cockiest egomaniac I had ever encountered. And I've met more than my share! But what Gary lacked in manners he more than made up for in intelligence. You couldn't question his IQ...and he wouldn't let you or anyone else forget it! He said he wanted me to put together a national Advertising program for the company, much the same as I had done for other companies needing to address the masses. Gary recognized that the ultimate success of his venture would be based on the ability to motivate consumers to visit not a building, but an Internet web site. There, they would have the opportunity to purchase common big-ticket items from the comfort of their living rooms, without ever stepping into a "brick and mortar" storefront. I agreed to jump on his bandwagon, whereupon he handed me a business plan the size of an encyclopedia to read that evening.

The more I read the plan, the more I had the gut instinct that something was very wrong with this picture. The entire premise of this new business was Gary's conviction that consumers would be willing to make a major purchase on-line, from a company they didn't know, without ever speaking to a person, for brand name products they could find at any big box store in any city in America. Gary was pinning his dreams on his belief (or hope) that consumers would indeed buy on-line as a means of saving money, since they would be able to buy the same products for less money than they could at a local store. You see, Gary's company would have no need for product inventory, warehouses, distribution centers, trucks, even employees, since all merchandise would be ordered on-line directly from the manufacturer, who would in turn ship directly to the purchasing consumer. The only record of the purchase would be the paper trail it had created. What continued to bother me was the thought of a consumer willingly paying by credit card over the Internet for products costing from hundreds to thousands of dollars, without ever seeing or touching the product, or even talking with a real live person. These were only a couple of the issues I would have to discuss with Gary in developing an effective Advertising strategy.

I met with Gary the next day and I raised the issues I just mentioned. He fluffed over them pretty quickly, for which there could only be two possible explanations. One, Gary knew that the very premise of this venture could not prove successful, but it didn't matter as long as he could convince venture capitalists to invest millions of dollars in it. Two, Gary was so overwhelmed with his idea that he really didn't or couldn't see the flaw. I'm convinced option #1 was the reality of the situation, especially since Gary had already successfully raised millions of dollars of venture capital to feed this Internet beast's voracious start-up appetite. The second day, I toured the Internet headquarters. With a lot of money behind it, the company was challenged to move quickly, before someone else came up with a better mousetrap, which instilled an unmistakable feeling of paranoia about the place. I spent the rest of the day in meetings with the people who were the brains behind the operation, at least technically, as well as the staff whose responsibility it was to secure working agreements with the national manufacturers whose products the company would represent and attempt to sell on-line. Everybody was duly excited about their financial prospects, considering the stock options that had been freely given to all employees. Although the concept of the Internet was as exciting as it was new, to me it was no different than any other media, be it TV or radio or the newspaper. You still had to follow certain guidelines, sometimes referred to as formulas for success or, in this book, **Secrets** of success! It didn't take me more than those first two days to understand that the very success of this venture would depend on the ability to convince consumers that this was the wave of the future. My most important challenge would be to create an Advertising program that would *motivate potential consumers to shop (and buy) from this place of business as opposed to someone else's.* Sound familiar? Yep, the good old premise of successful Advertising, as presented to you in the **Introduction**. It hasn't yet changed, and it probably never will! In this case, the only variable that had changed was the medium.

The plan I developed was actually quite simple, as most good plans are. If you'll recall, I've been telling you all along that *Advertising isn't brain surgery!* The essence of my proposal was a cost-efficient, region-by-region cable-TV campaign, supported by national print ads, inviting consumers to visit the web site, where they would be able to buy products they were going to purchase anyway, but at spectacular savings compared to the old way of buying at their local store. It's really a very old approach to a very old problem: Convenience + savings + brand name credibility = success. Of course, my job was to add some excitement, as well! To my way of thinking, this approach was no different than convincing consumers to shop at any other place of business to get the savings they valued on the products they wanted. The only difference was that this place of business was located not down the street, but inside their own computers! On the third day, I presented my proposal to Gary and his managers, not even for a moment thinking there was anything that could be argued. Wrong again!

Gary exploded out of his chair, eager to impress the assembled guests with the extent of his genius IQ. "Don't you understand?" he assaulted.

"Our customers are not the same people who might be swayed by your car commercials, or your furniture commercials, or your carpet commercials, or any other commercials! Our customers are different! For one thing, they don't watch TV! For another, they certainly won't respond to the same old techniques of advertising that you're proposing!" Did you ever find yourself in the position of feeling the heat rise in your cheeks, and no matter how hard you concentrated on it, you couldn't prevent them from turning red? "If the truth be known," I attempted to interject, "the people we need to reach are the very same people who are out buying cars, furniture, carpet, or anything else. Just because you want them to buy over the Internet instead of…" Gary interrupted me in a rush, "Our shoppers will be educated professionals in the upper echelons of society, certainly not the kind of people who would be influenced by the old ways of doing things. Is this the best you can offer?" I now had a choice. I could argue my point with a tyrant, or I could sit down, defeated. I chose neither. Instead, I smiled, packed my proposal into my briefcase, strode up to Gary, shook his hand, and wished him bon chance. I then politely thanked those assembled for their kind attention and left, a mere three days into my "can't miss" Internet opportunity! As I departed, I noticed that the managers looked as if they themselves agreed with me, but were too intimidated by Gary's ego to speak out. It came as no surprise that within a year, despite many millions of dollars invested, this dot-com had gone dot-bust. The sad part is that Gary was undoubtedly successful in walking away with millions of dollars before the bottom dropped out. So, from his perspective, I suppose it was a successful business venture. As usual, there are lessons to be learned in every situation. We now know that the Internet can be a valuable tool for building your business, in conjunction with other tools. The *tools* may change, but the *rules* don't. By all means, use the Internet for what it does best. But you would be well advised not to do so at the expense of everything else you do in Advertising your business. Think of it as another TV station, another radio station, just another one of **My Favorite Things.** (Thank you, Richard Rodgers!)

LET SOMEONE ELSE DO IT

If someone gives you the advice, "Let someone else do it," chances are that someone is lazy. But not always! This advice was first offered to me by Mike, a car dealership owner who has been my client for fifteen years at the time of this writing. Having worked with hundreds of car dealers, I can tell you that many of them are…well…*unique* individuals. Most are tough negotiators, as they have to be. Some are abrupt, impolite, harsh, and downright nasty! But I've enjoyed working with car dealers more than owners in any other business category, probably because they always laughed at my jokes, which doesn't speak too highly of their sense of humor.

What struck me the first time I stepped into Mike's office was the large picture hanging on the wall behind his desk, a framed ink drawing depicting the face of a man with the biggest, happiest smile you can imagine. On second glance, the man in the picture looked familiar, with scruffy beard and long, over-the-shoulder hair. I was mesmerized by this picture, and asked Mike about it. Mike was a deacon in his church, and a deeply religious man. He explained that the picture was a modern representation of Jesus, and served as his daily reminder that his Lord was, above all else, a man on earth, like other men, with happiness and the love of life at the core of His being. This was quite a contrast to the crucified Christ on the cross, or the Pieta's Christ in the arms of Mary, that we are so accustomed to seeing portrayed in religiously inspired art. Mike and I spent the next hour discussing religion, philosophy, life, and anything else totally unrelated to selling cars. What began in Mike's office that day became, over the years, a deep mutual respect, a friendship that transcends the daily grind of the business world. I don't mind telling you that at a particularly trying time for me, Mike counseled me with this advice: "The Lord is at your side, even if you can't see Him." I'm not of the Christian faith, and frankly, I was unaccustomed to that tone of conversation, but I graciously accepted the advice with a nod. Months later, I told Mike how the situation that had caused me so much concern had seemingly resolved itself. He looked at me, smiled, and said, "I told you, the Lord is at your side. Sometimes, you just can't see His hand until you look back. Then you realize that He was there, guiding you, all along." At that moment, selling cars was the furthest thing from my mind.

Mike had hired me as his Advertising agent because of my growing reputation as someone who could successfully create promotional excitement at a car dealership. Mike had taken over the reigns at his dealership after the death of his father, who had founded the business in the early fifties. The dealership was grounded in a decades-long tradition of unparalleled customer service, rather than hyped sales promotions. However, given the hard economic times, it became essential to the survival of many businesses that you do things differently, or risk not surviving the business consolidation movement that was sweeping the nation. As we discussed strategies for increasing consumer traffic in his showroom, Mike continually harkened back to his strong belief in the necessity of maintaining his hard-earned reputation as a customer service leader through the use of customer testimonials. I had no experience in this area, and tried to let Mike's words "go in one ear and out the other." But he insisted the best approach for his dealership would be a combination of strong promotions and customer testimonials. Although I wasn't sold on the concept it was, after all, Mike's dealership we were talking about, and his money that was being invested in Advertising!

I asked Mike why he was so set on this idea of testimonials. And that's when he gave me the advice that is the title of this chapter. He was convinced that it was much more meaningful for someone else to talk about how good your business was, rather than say it yourself. Many car dealers were appearing in their own TV commercials in an endless variety of false settings, reading the standard "we're so wonderful" ad copy written for them by their ad agents, and pretending to believe it! Mike held firm to his belief that Joe Customer would be his best spokesperson. "I'd rather let my customers talk about the good experience they had at my dealership, Jeff. It's real, and it's credible. People believe other people." After taking a look at some of the testimonial ads Mike had previously used, I believed I could make them better, and I made some recommendations in that regard, from the production standpoint. "We need to dress these ads up," I said. "Let's use professional actors instead of the customers themselves. The ads will look more professional and slick." Mike firmly held his ground, insisting that what made them so effective was the very fact that they were delivered by actual customers, in the showroom, unrehearsed, talking about their positive personal experiences at the dealership. As I've suggested in earlier chapters, good ad agents learn to listen, and present their ideas in such a way as to suggest that the ideas were in fact the client's ideas. Mike had certainly turned the tables on me! He let me think that this concept of "real people" advertising was mine. Shame on you, Mike. Now, years later, I've asked Mike what the secret to our long working relationship has been. He's quick to respond, "You were willing to take my ideas, combine them with yours, and incorporate them into an effective advertising program. And you did it without making me feel like my own ideas weren't important." If Mike only knew that what I valued was his willingness to accept my ideas in a way that didn't make me feel like he thought his ideas were more important than mine!

In the chapter **Who Am I to Tell You, Anyway**, I told you about leaving the brutal cold, constant snow, and depressing gray skies of Western New York in favor of sunny, small-town Virginia. A few weeks before we were to depart, my wife asked me if I had said anything to Mike yet. You know, it hadn't even dawned on me. We had worked together for so long that I didn't even consider not continuing a working relationship with Mike, even though I would be some 750 miles away. It was strange, but to the clients I had worked with over the years in my hometown, I was just their local "ad guy." They either didn't know, or didn't care, that I had in fact developed a nationally syndicated company, working from a distance with literally thousands of business owners all over the country. Heeding my wife's wise counsel, I called Mike and invited him to one of our usual Advertising power lunches. As always, we went to Bill Grey's, a hot dog stand not far from Mike's dealership! Mike got his usual two dogs with hot sauce and fries, and I got my usual Grilled Cheese and tomato sandwich. I always got a kick out of the fact that Mike seemed to feel guilty letting me pay for our power lunch, which never exceeded $12. And I didn't even put it on a company credit card! The gentleman he is, Mike always insisted that we end our lunch at the neighborhood ice cream parlor, where he would buy dessert. Anyway, I never anticipated having any difficulty telling Mike that I was leaving Rottenchester in favor of a warmer clime. But there I sat, avoiding the discussion with every bite of lunch. If you recall, in **Choose Your Bed Mates Carefully**, I likened the agency/client relationship to marriage. The longer I procrastinated, the more difficult it became. I'm sure Mike sensed my uneasiness, because after lunch we just sat looking out the window, not saying much, he waiting for me to get something off my chest. "Mike…there's something I need to tell you," I stammered. By the stricken look on his face, I suspect Mike was anticipating that I was about ready to demand a divorce! But he just waited, not wanting to interrupt my thoughts. I went on to explain that I had decided to pull up stakes and move south, not just for the winter, but permanently, and that I wanted to cut way back on my business activities. I concluded by telling him that I hoped our personal friendship would continue, as well as our business relationship, explaining that I would feel privileged to serve as his ad agent from my new Virginia home. It may be hard for you to understand, but I had great difficulty not choking up as I spoke, and I'm sure my eyes were watery. But I got it out. Mike paused, then turned his head away towards the window and said, "I envy your decision." I guess that broke the ice, because we spoke about life and family for another half-hour before diving into our ice cream dessert down the road. As far as our working relationship, Mike expressed the one concern he had, whether I could continue to provide the same excellent personal service from 750 miles away that I had provided as his local ad guy. I reminded him that 99% of my clients during the past years had in fact been people in other towns, people that I rarely met with personally. He said, "Let's see how it goes." Three months later, I asked Mike how it had been going, and he answered, "Jeff, I don't understand it, but you service me better from 750 miles away than you ever did right here in town! How can that be?" I laughed. "The answer is simple…ego. I've always prided myself on the ability to provide excellent service from afar. You were just never afar, Mike!"

Advertising is so much more than Art or Science. It's all about People, and how they interact. And when you're offered the advice to let someone else do it? When it comes to customer testimonials, **It's All Right With Me.** (Thanks yet again, Cole Porter!)

TRY SOMETHING NEW

I had just conducted a spirited seminar in Las Vegas for the benefit of small business owners, about increasing the effectiveness of their local Advertising efforts. Max approached me later in the cafeteria, introduced himself, and asked if he might join me for lunch. "Pull up a chair," I insisted. After a bit of small talk, Max explained that he owned a retail store in rural Alabama. He had owned his store for more years than I could include at my last birthday, and he wasn't too proud or ashamed to acknowledge his need for some help in getting it back into a position of profitability, and his hope of injecting new life into his stagnant business. "Maybe this dog is just too old for any new tricks, but I'm willing to try whatever you recommend," he confided. Max just looked so defeated that my heart ached. On the business road, every once in a while you meet someone who reaches out and captures your concern, and Max certainly caught mine. Having lived my entire life in the Northeast, I had heard that Southerners were, by nature, polite. But Max displayed so much more than the typical Southern gentility. The problem with developing a personal liking for a client is that you inevitably place a heavy burden on your shoulders, knowing that convincing him to follow your advice could well determine the very fate of his business in the near future. Give the right advice, and you're a hero. Give the wrong advice, and you're nothing but a great pretender to the throne of Advertising expert.

This was late November, and Max wanted to get the ball rolling quickly. I told him that I thought the ideal time to introduce "the new Max" to his community would be New Year's Day, during a gala New Year's Day Sale, complete with complimentary champagne. "New Year's

Day? No one in our area is open New Year's Day. And besides, I'd feel guilty asking my staff to work on a holiday!" During the seminar, I had spent some time talking about many of the things I'm mentioning in this book, including "throwing a party at your place of business." I proceeded to explain to Max that I believed he needed to throw a party at his store, and invite the public as his guests. And what better time to make a new beginning than on New Year's Day? Just between you and me, I felt pretty secure in offering Max this advice, since New Year's Day sales were as close to guaranteed success as you could predict, assuming you advertised the event properly! I continued my wise counsel by telling Max that he only needed to open for a few hours, in the afternoon. "A few hours? I can't imagine being able to do enough business in just a few hours!" I told Max that I would research the media costs in his market and get back to him within a few days. As luck would have it, my research showed that Max was indeed fortunate to be located in a small town that had its own TV station, and it was an ABC affiliate, to boot! Furthermore, we could saturate the airwaves on New Year's Eve for a "paltry" $1,500. I was so excited, I immediately called Max in Alabama. "$1,500, Jeff? That's more than I spent all of last *year* on advertising!" What Max didn't realize (until I told him) was that the exact same schedule of TV spots that would cost $1,500 in his small town would cost $150,000 if his store had been located in New York City! I guess that's all Max needed to hear, because he told me to go forward and book the airtime for him.

Over the next couple of weeks, I put the finishing touches on Max's New Year's Day Sale. I called him in late December just to make sure he hadn't changed his mind, and he sounded so excited. I asked him about it, and he said, "Well, Jeff, I enjoyed your seminar, and I sure heard what you said about throwing a party at my store, so that's exactly what I'm gonna do! Our sale starts at 1 o'clock on New Year's Day, but I'm throwing my party at 11 that morning!" I was confused, to say the least. "Max, how can you throw your party at 11 if the sale doesn't start until one?" His answer stunned me. "Well, Jeff, I felt so guilty asking my staff to work New Year's Day, I'm throwing the party for them at 11. I hired a caterer to bring in a full brunch, Southern style, and a band to play some down-home fiddle music! And the band members said they'd stay and play all afternoon if I wanted, as long as I fed 'em." I was about to tell Max that he had misunderstood my advice, that the word "party" was meant in a figurative sense, and intended for the customers, not the staff. Before embarrassing myself by speaking up, it occurred to me that Max had in fact taken my idea of "throwing a party" for his customers to its logical conclusion by using it as a well deserved reward for his staff. And to think Max was worried about teaching an old dog new tricks! In this case, I readily admit it was the young dog learning a new trick. "Great idea, Max! I'm glad I thought of it! Listen, I'll call you after the sale to see how it went. Happy New Year."

I didn't have to call Max after his sale. He called me on January 2nd. No, Max didn't "pull an Irwin" on me. He was too polite. But he did draw the story out over the better part of an hour before finally telling me his sales results, which were pretty spectacular. Max went on to explain that the biggest problem they faced New Year's Day happened around noon. Again, I was totally confused! "Max, what could have happened at noon? Your employee party was at 11, and the store didn't open until one, so what am I missing here?" Max took great pleasure in the yarn he then spun. "Well, Jeff, we started our party in the store right at 11 in the morning. To be perfectly honest with you, none of us, me included, expected anything worth writing home about, but we were all having fun nonetheless. The food was wonderful, and the band had everyone up dancin' to the tunes. Then, at around noon, we all heard these strange noises coming from up in front of the store. Since our party was set up in the back storeroom, we couldn't see what was causin' all the ruckus, so we moseyed up to the front showroom. And can you believe it? It looked like half the town was pounding on our front door, wantin' to get in on the fun. So, we opened up the doors an hour early, and in they flocked! The sale was supposed to be over by 5, but everyone just stayed 'til around 7 or 8, we wuz all havin' such a grand old time." My smile must have lit up my office, I was so happy for Max. There was only one thing I thought to ask him before hanging up the phone. "But Max, did you sell any merchandise?" As only an Alabaman could, he answered, "Oh heck, we did that, too!"

To this day, I don't know what I would have done if Max's New Year's Day Sale had been a flop. And it's a good thing he didn't "pull an Irwin" on me, because I think I would have suffered a stroke on the spot. A week later, I received the most delightful letter from Max, admitting that he really had expected a crowd…but not a stampede! The lesson to be learned is simple. Try something new. The worst thing that could happen is that it might not work. The best thing is that it might. What do you have to lose, except maybe, $1,500? This was one time I was overjoyed to be a hero, **More Than You Know.** (Thank you, Vincent Youmans!)

YOU'RE PROBABLY WONDERING

You're probably wondering if there's one question that always got asked at every seminar I've ever conducted. Then again, maybe you're not wondering that at all. Hmm, I guess **I Can't Get Started.** (Thank you, Vernon Duke!)

TO ADVERTISE OR TO SELL,
THAT IS THE QUESTION

Now that you've had a moment to think about it, you know this could be a very important question! Yes, there is one question that's always asked. Question: Should you advertise what you sell, or sell what you advertise? Answer: No! Wait a minute, how can that be? If I shouldn't advertise what I wish to sell, and if I shouldn't sell what I wish to advertise, then what? In virtually every book ever written about the game of Advertising, you'll likely be introduced to the example of the super market that advertises a quart of milk at a price far below what milk usually sells for. The whole idea is to motivate the consumer to shop at the market, recognizing the value of the advertised special. This is called *Loss Leader Advertising*. The premise is very simple. The market advertises this product at or below its cost, knowing they will lose money, or at the least not make money, every time this product is purchased. Why do they do it? I assure you, it's not because they are kind hearted. They do it because they expect you probably won't leave their market without buying much more than just the milk that is advertised as a loss leader. As a matter of fact, you'll notice that the dairy section is probably located at the very far corner of the store, "forcing" you to walk the aisles before you locate the advertised special. As you walk those aisles, the market is counting on you to pick up a bag of chips, hot dogs and buns, mustard and ketchup, a liter of pop (soda), and whatever else happens to find its way into your cart "when you're not looking." Oh, sure, one or two smart shoppers will just buy the milk and leave without buying anything else, but their numbers are so insignificant in the scope of the market's everyday business that a few pennies lost aren't even noticed. What's that? You say this is fine for a super market, but you don't own a super market? Read on, please!

After another of my Advertising workshops, this one in Atlanta, a business owner asked if I would meet with him over coffee to discuss his dilemma. While it doesn't matter to the example, I'll tell you that he owned a floor covering business in a mid-Atlantic state, catering not to the general public but to builders. In fact, his showroom wasn't even open to the public! Over the years, Art had built a very successful business, serving the needs of home-builders and contractors who looked to buy his floor covering products at a substantial discount in exchange for their guaranteed volume purchasing. As is always the case, things change! On one side, new home construction had fallen off dramatically, thereby reducing Art's bottom line. On the other, more and more retail carpet stores were looking to the builder market to prop up their own sagging sales. As a result, Art found himself in the very uncomfortable position of needing to change his method of operation, indeed his very thought process, if he wished to survive the changing economic climate. As you may know, change isn't easy. During our meeting, Art confessed that although he had thoroughly enjoyed my seminar presentation, he felt totally lost and out of place, since his had never been a retail store, and he didn't even know where to start the process of addressing the general public. In other words, he had never before experienced the need to advertise. As you might expect, there were just too many issues beyond the Advertising challenge that Art needed to address, and this couldn't be accomplished in a casual meeting over coffee. So Art and I agreed that I would assist him in structuring an effective Advertising strategy, and he would necessarily have to endure a learn-as-you-go process in terms of the retail business side of the equation. Mistakes would be made. As predicted, the result of our first promotional effort had both a positive and a negative outcome. I'll tell you about both, in the hope you'll learn from each.

I shouldn't admit this to you, but the media side of the strategy was easy. Once you've done something enough times, you can't help but become reasonably good at it. So, my plan for an introductory promotional sales event at Art's showroom quickly fell into place with his acceptance of my media plan, which called for TV and newspaper Advertising. Then it was time to get into the nitty gritty of the ads themselves, what we would say, and how we would say it. Knowing what Art's reaction would be before I even uttered a word, I recommended that we advertise a price point of $8.99 sq./yd., which was attractive enough to generate consumer interest. As expected, Art objected. "Jeff, I don't sell any $8.99 goods. I don't even have any. And frankly, I don't want to sell $8.99 carpet. We carry only premium goods, more in the range of $40 and up. That's what I want to sell." I answered his objection, knowing it was coming before he had even vocalized it. "Art, I know you don't sell $8.99 carpet, and I know you don't want to. I'm not asking you to *sell* $8.99 carpet, I'm suggesting you *advertise* $8.99 carpet. If we advertise $40 carpet, which is what you want to sell, not one person will come into your showroom to see it. The first thing you need to do is get your hands on some merchandise that you can legitimately offer at $8.99. Go to the mills, buy up some close-outs and end cuts, buy some remnants, buy some off colors, buy anything that you can offer at, or even slightly below your cost, to get us to that $8.99 price point. In my opinion, that's the magic number." After a moment or two of silent contemplation, Art answered, "OK, I'm listening. But what am I gonna do with this stuff? I sure don't want to sell anything below cost!" I explained to Art that we would use it as *Advertising fodder*. If you remember, effective Advertising is based on *motivating potential consumers to shop (and buy) at your place of business, rather than someone else's.* Let's address the *shop* part first. The use of *Advertising fodder* is specifically designed to do one thing only, that being to entice people to come into your store based on a perceived value. And the reality of the perception in this case is that the $8.99

merchandise *is* indeed a great value, since you're pricing it at or below your cost! Do you want to sell it? Of course you don't. But you need to advertise it to accomplish the first part of the equation, enticing consumers into your store. Now, let's address the *buy* part. If you remember nothing else in this chapter, remember this piece of advice! *Advertising* can't sell your product...*People* sell it! "Selling up" has been a common practice in business since the dawn of mankind. That's why you hire good sales people as opposed to order takers. There's no question that the majority of consumers who respond to Art's ad will be disappointed in the $8.99 carpet for a number of reasons. "It's not the right color," or "the quality isn't what I had in mind." Remember, its sole purpose is to entice the consumer into Art's store, where it will be the sales agent's job to sell to that consumer the carpet that Art and everyone else know from the get-go the consumer wants to buy anyway, the $40 stuff!

Art's next question was also anticipated. "Jeff, isn't that Bait and Switch?" That question raises one of the most misunderstood issues in Advertising. By it's very nature and purpose, Advertising is the bait the retailer puts on his hook to lure the consumer to his spot on the pond. It's morally acceptable, it's ethical, and it's a standard business practice recognized by consumers. The problem lies not in the *Bait*, but in the *Switch*. Even though you don't really want to sell the $8.99 carpet to your customers, if someone wishes to buy it you must sell it. Is that so difficult? The worst thing you can do is either refuse to sell it, or substitute a lesser quality product in its place after the sale. That *is* Bait and Switch. And that's illegal. Art was beginning to understand the process, and agreed to lay hands on the necessary fodder. There were many other issues Art and I discussed over the next weeks, but for the purposes of this chapter, everything was now in place for his first effort at reaching out to the general public, a two-day sales event on Friday and Saturday. I called Art on the Monday morning after the event, and I was told he couldn't come to the phone. The same occurred on

Monday afternoon, Tuesday morning, and Tuesday afternoon. Finally, on Wednesday afternoon, Art called me. You've probably already guessed why he couldn't come to the phone Monday or Tuesday. Yes, he was swamped. In recounting the events of the past weekend, Art was simply overwhelmed by the numbers. During the two-day sales event, 115 customers had visited the showroom. (That's exceptional!) I did some quick mental calculations, knowing that the average ticket sale in a carpet store was between $800 and $1,000. Art went on to say that they had closed a high percentage of the customers, in the 80% range, which I figured into my calculation. At this point, I was pretty sure Art had realized about a 25:1 return on his investment (see **Concentrate Your Efforts**), which also is exceptional, especially the first time out of the box. But when I asked him for the final sales figure, the number he gave me was well below what it should have been. Something was wrong, and Art didn't even realize it yet, he was so taken aback by the sheer numbers. If you go back a few paragraphs, I had warned Art *mistakes would be made*. And this mistake needed investigation to prevent it from happening again.

Art and I proceeded to play twenty questions. It seemed he had done everything right in purchasing the necessary *Advertising fodder*. On the surface, it appeared his sales staff was well prepared, given the 80% closing ratio. The number of consumers entering the store, 115, should have generated a much higher sales volume than the figure Art quoted me. Unable to think of anything else, I asked Art to talk me through the sales process, from the customer's perspective. His answer uncovered the problem pretty quickly. "Let's see, Jeff…whenever a customer came in, we would approach and offer assistance…most people said they wanted to see the advertised specials, so we would walk them back into the warehouse…" Oops. I jumped in with the question I already knew the answer to. "Art, why did you walk them back into the warehouse?" He replied, "because that's where we unloaded all the specials we had bought for the sale, you know, the $8.99 goods." My heart sank. "Art, why did you put all the *Advertising fodder* in the warehouse, far removed from the rest of the merchandise in your showroom?" He answered slowly, beginning to realize what had happened. "Well…it just wasn't up to par with our normal stock, so we figured we'd feel better if it wasn't out in plain sight in the showroom…big mistake, right?" And there it was. The whole idea was to mix that merchandise in with the running stock, "forcing" the consumer to stroll the aisles. More importantly, the visual difference in quality between the advertised specials and the running stock would have made it so much easier for the sales person to sell up to a better quality product. By removing all the specials from the showroom, in fact walking the customers back to the warehouse, Art had inadvertently made it all too easy for the consumer to buy the advertised specials without ever being introduced to the merchandise he really wanted to sell to them! Even though it appeared at first that the sales staff had done their job, in reality they were prevented from doing it by the very procedure they followed. The high closing ratio of 80% was, unfortunately, a direct result of selling the advertised specials, which was not the goal. The good news is that once Art and his staff got the hang of it, they were more successful in subsequent events, achieving their sales goals on a regular basis.

If you've patiently read this chapter to this point, even though you're not in the floor covering business, the same philosophy holds true in virtually any business category. Why does the furniture store advertise a two-for-one special on recliners? Is it because they want to sell recliners at half-price? Or is it because they hope you'll be enticed into the store by this advertised special, and you'll end up buying a bedroom set, or a living room suite, with or without the recliners? Why does the appliance store advertise a $39 microwave? Is it because they want to sell one to you? Or is it because you'll end up buying the $449 model which has the wattage you really need and want? Why does the car dealer advertise a stripped-down base model at the lowest price possible? Is it because they want to sell you that vehicle? Or is it because they know that once you test drive the model with power steering, power brakes, power locks, and all the other goodies, that's the one you'll end up wanting? Why does the clothing store advertise cashmere sweaters at $99? Is it because they want to sell you a $99 cashmere sweater? Or is it because they know you'll end up buying the $399 sweater that's available in the color you want, unlike the advertised special which is only available in lime green? Rest assured, by following this chapter's advice regarding selling versus advertising, you certainly **Ain't Misbehavin'**. (Thank you, Fats Waller!)

IT TAKES THREE TO TANGO

Perhaps the one feature of my agency most loved by its sales agents was the "open commission" structure I dreamed up. The beauty of syndication is the ability to work with any business owner, anywhere in the country, without geographic restriction. So I instituted a policy for the account executives that enabled them to stick me for the bill for not only their vacation, but their spending money, as well! It was standard procedure for the company to send agents out on a weekly basis to several cities, with the company footing the bill for all travel and lodging. On top of that, the sales commission paid to the agents was substantial. Quite simply, I invited any interested agents to devote the first day of their vacation to making a sales presentation or two in whatever city they were visiting. If successful, the agency would pay their travel expenses for the vacation, plus the standard commission. This program turned out to be strong motivation, particularly for the wives of the agents. "You get out there and make Jeff pay for our vacation!" Such was the case for this example of an agent securing an account on his first vacation day in Florida. The very first car dealership he visited signed up to run *The World's Greatest Car Sale* (see **Grab Their Attention**). By 11 o'clock on the first morning of vacation, my agent and his wife knew they could enjoy the rest of their week on the house, so to speak.

We went through the usual preparations in developing the media plan and producing the necessary materials, faxing the customary printed directions to the dealer, which explained the ins and outs of the event and how to properly prepare for it. By this time, the production process had begun to resemble a factory assembly line, and we kept the crank turning as often and efficiently as possible. The only problem with the new efficiency is that you sometimes might not notice the little warning signs that used to be evident in the "old" way of doing things, talking a client through the process step-by-step over the phone. On the weekend of Kurt's sales event in Florida, we probably had at least 25 other car dealers running the same event in 25 other cities. In the early days, it had been my practice to make the Monday-morning-after-the-sale phone call to the client to talk about the results. But with so many clients, that responsibility had fallen to the executive in charge of the account. On this day, the AE came flying into my office, virtually begging that I take over and handle a nasty situation. "What's the problem?" I asked. He gave me a 30-second summary while Kurt was on hold, whereupon I punched in on the flashing line to be greeted by Kurt, the car dealer in Florida. "So! You're the guy, are you? Well let me tell you, that garbage you sold me wasn't worth a quart of owl pee!" That was a new one I'd never heard before. My mind started wandering with visions of owls doing what Kurt had suggested, and I just couldn't picture it. Do owls pee? I've never seen it happen! But back to Kurt's call. One thing I had learned over the years was the necessity of listening, and allowing a disgruntled person (client or not) the courtesy of venting before I responded (see **Listen to Everyone**). Kurt continued on the warpath for a good ten minutes. (Actually, it was quite a bad ten minutes.) When he had finally relieved himself of all hostility, I said, "Kurt, I'm truly sorry for the negative outcome you just described. While it won't solve the problem totally, I'd like to offer you a full refund on the fee you paid for our event. Having said that, may I ask if you'd be kind enough to talk me through the event, day by day?" Suddenly, Kurt was Mr. Polite, and replied, "Sure, Jeff. There's really not much to tell. Bottom line, we didn't sell any cars!" I wasn't about to accuse Kurt of fibbing, so I continued my line of questioning. "Humph, that's terrible. Let me ask you this, Kurt. How many customers would you say came in on each of the four days of the event?" I suspected I knew what his answer would be, but it was important for Kurt to verbalize it. "Customers? Hell, Jeff, we had more dad-gum customers than I've ever seen here, but they weren't buyers. They were just tire kickers!" And there it was. Read any book on Advertising and somewhere it'll make the point that Advertising can be expected to do no more than drive the consumers into the store. The rest is up to the business owner and his employees. By definition, the Advertising must be considered successful if it accomplishes it's sole function, that being to *motivate the consumer to shop (and buy) at your place of business.* I wasn't about to tell Kurt that by definition this had been a successful promotion, since it had indeed motivated consumers to *shop* at his dealership! And I wasn't about to tell him that he had dropped the ball on the *buy* half of the equation. But we did spend the next half-hour talking about his sales staff, his inventory, his pricing, and a host of other business topics that an Advertising maven isn't supposed to even know about, let alone understand.

Two things were readily apparent. First, the sales staff had fallen down. Kurt admitted, "a few of my best guys were off that weekend." We talked about the need to have everyone on board, on the same page, hungry for a major event to be successful. Then we discussed the rest of the sales staff. I was left with a very disturbing vision of the old, burned-out car salesman, beer gut hanging out over too tight plaid pants, reclining with feet up on the desk, addressing a customer with a "Yea, can I help you?" Finally, Kurt actually admitted that even he wasn't at the dealership the first three days of the event, more eager to play some golf at the club. Even worse, neither he nor any member of his staff had bothered to read our printed instructions prior to the event. Ever so slowly and methodically, the revelations couldn't help but make their point. I didn't have to say much, just ask the questions. Kurt then confessed another sin! His inventory for the sale wasn't anywhere near what it should have been. In fact, he was already experiencing a shortage of vehicles, unable to get delivery from the factory. When you add an inadequate selection of vehicles to an inadequate sales staff, you don't have to be a genius to know why the event didn't meet Kurt's unrealistic expectations. By the end of our conversation, I wouldn't say Kurt and I had become bosom-buddies, but we did understand each other. The last thing he said before we disconnected was "I'm really sorry I flew off the handle like that. And the refund you offered? I appreciate it, but it wouldn't be right. You earned your money."

Advertising is only one of the three building blocks in the foundation of a successful event, indeed a successful business. The other two are Merchandising and Selling. In this case, the Merchandising block refers to Kurt's inventory of vehicles, how they were priced, how they were presented on the lot and in the showroom. The Selling block refers to Kurt's sales staff, how well they were trained, how motivated they were, and the sales approach and process they followed. Without all three building blocks in place and rock solid, the foundation will be irreparably weakened, and the building will sway, if not crumble. Think of it this way. Imagine you have the Merchandising and Selling blocks in place. If the Advertising block is missing or weak, the consumers won't shop your place of business, no matter how many cars you have to sell, and no matter how good your sales staff! Next, imagine you have the Merchandising and Advertising blocks in place. If your Selling block is absent or weak, the consumers won't be sold. Finally, imagine you have the Selling and Advertising blocks in place. If the Merchandising block is absent or weak, you can't succeed for want of inventory to sell. In Kurt's case, I respectfully suggest he had the best Advertising block money could buy, but he had weak Merchandising and Selling blocks, accounting for the dismal results of his event, indeed his overall business. Yes, it takes three to Tango **On the Street Where You Live.** (Thank you, Frederick Loewe!)

POLITICS

Kevin approached me after attending a seminar I conducted at a national trade show, this one in San Francisco. Like so many other small business owners, he and his family had purchased a business franchise two years prior, in the hope that they might be spared the joys of the dreaded GOB Sale. As we sat and talked over lunch, Kevin vented his world of problems relating to the very premise of franchising. Theoretically, franchising is a marvelous concept, not all that different from the Advertising cookie cutter concept I described in this book's chapter, **Who Am I to Tell You, Anyway?** In the case of Kevin and his family, their business had been reasonably successful for a number of years prior to their decision to purchase a franchise. However, as the business consolidation movement swept the nation, they found it increasingly difficult, if not impossible in their own eyes, to compete with the many new, well-funded franchise operations that were taking business away from them right in their local marketplace. So they searched for the franchise they thought would best suit their needs, one that would give them the national clout they couldn't seem to muster as a local Mom-and-Pop business. They were promised all variety of assistance in exchange for their substantial franchise fee. For example, they were sold on the premise of the hefty monetary savings to be realized through the volume purchasing power the franchiser exercised over its supplying manufacturers. Beyond monetary issues, Kevin placed a high value on the opportunity to network with like business owners in other cities. Perhaps most important, Kevin was convinced that his participation in a focused Advertising program developed by the franchiser for the benefit of its franchisees would attract local customers more cost-efficiently than he could ever hope to attract as a stand-alone business. What Kevin got for his hard-earned investment was much different than the promises made. For one thing, it soon became apparent that any financial benefit of volume purchasing was lost in the franchise royalties Kevin paid on his gross sales. To add insult to injury, the franchiser was extremely loose in its definition of market exclusivity, selling franchises to other business owners in Kevin's marketplace. As a result, Kevin and family now had to compete not only with other local businesses, but also with their own franchise company! The network they established with other franchisees in other cities turned out to be nothing more than a forum for all the complaints the franchisees had, and couldn't seem to do anything about. Last and certainly not least, the Advertising program that had been developed by the franchiser was not only out-dated, but also poorly planned and executed. Put another way, it didn't *motivate potential consumers to shop (and buy)* at Kevin's place of business. Kevin felt he could live with all the other problems if he had to, but not the Advertising, which he recognized as the very life-blood of his business. Unfortunately, with regards to the Advertising issue, the fine print in Kevin's franchise agreement stated that he was legally obligated to use only the franchiser's Advertising program, and failure to do so could result in severe financial penalties and forfeiture of his franchise. Kevin concluded his tirade by throwing his hands in the air and pleading, "What do I do now? If things keep going the way they're going, we'll be out of business within a year." I could sympathize with Kevin's dilemma, but I wondered aloud how I could be of any assistance in nudging him over this seemingly insurmountable hurdle. He answered in a most complimentary tone of voice, "I paid very close attention to everything you said in your seminar. Frankly, the examples you demonstrated were far superior to the ads we have no choice but to buy from our own franchise company's in-house ad agency. They won't listen to us, so I'm going to do whatever I have to do to save by business, franchise or not." With that, Kevin asked me to become his ad agency of record, despite the risk he ran of being in violation of his franchise agreement. "I just don't want you spreading the word, Jeff, if you know what I mean."

Within a couple of weeks, Kevin and his family business became another of my "clone cookies" (see **Who Am I to Tell You, Anyway?**). After only six months of working together, Kevin confided that the simple act of switching to my Advertising program had yielded an unbelievable 40% increase in gross sales at his store, without any increase in Advertising expenditures. Kevin now commanded a position of relative dominance in his marketplace, and we continued our agency/client relationship for several years. Despite my pride in the results of our efforts, I remained true to my word and kept my mouth shut! As you probably already know, the business community is really quite small, and just as tightly knit. It didn't take long before I started getting calls from other disgruntled franchisees after hearing about Kevin's success through their networking grapevine. Before I turned around, I was working with Kevin's "cousins" in various cities across the country. And that's when I received another one of those unpleasant phone calls, this one from the director of the in-house ad agency for the franchiser. To this day, I don't understand why so many business people seem to think intimidation and nastiness are required to make a point (see **Listen to Everyone**). But I endured his unflinching reading of the riot act, since I didn't have another choice other than hanging up on him. In reality, this man had no power over me, since I had done nothing wrong. Unfortunately, he did have power over Kevin, and made no attempt to hide his intention to sue Kevin for damages, contending that his violation of the franchise agreement had resulted in a substantial loss of Advertising revenue to his in-house ad agency. I had only one hope of salvaging this situation. As diplomatically as possible, I suggested that Kevin and the other franchisees had jumped on my wagon for one reason. They were apparently dissatisfied with what they had, and found something better. I concluded by offering my services and proven programs to the franchiser on a freelance basis. This solution would have allowed these disgruntled franchisees to continue utilizing my services without being in violation of their agreement, and furthermore would have provided the in-house agency a vehicle for increasing its revenues by offering my programs to the rest of the franchisees on a commissioned basis. Suffice it to say the gentleman didn't (choose to) see any benefit in my proposal. Two weeks later, I received in the mail the required termination of service letters from all the involved franchisees. As spokesperson for the group, Kevin called to explain that the franchiser had indeed initiated legal proceedings against them, such action to be dropped only upon their termination of a working relationship with any outside Advertising sources.

Purchasing a franchise or joining a cooperative buying group may prove a wonderful growth opportunity for your business. Then again, it may not! The example of Kevin is meant as a warning to do your homework, which includes reading and understanding the fine print before signing away your rights. Weigh the advantages and the disadvantages of your decision. Most important, talk to as many franchisees or group members as feasible *before* you make your final decision. It could save you not only money, but also some unnecessary **Stormy Weather**. (Thank you, Harold Arlen!)

SOMEONE, SOMEWHERE, WILL COMPLAIN

It's a hard lesson to learn, but no matter how you try not to offend anyone, someone, somewhere, will complain about your Advertising! Be aware of this, but don't spend too much time worrying about it, because that will prevent you from being effective and creative in the long run. In the end, how you handle the problem will determine whether you've made a valued friend or a lifelong enemy. I'd like to give you two examples that I encountered. I think you'll get a kick out of these.

I received literally a last-minute desperation phone call from a car dealer I had worked with over the years. Through a rather amusing twist of events, he had managed to get a Hollywood celebrity who was visiting town to agree to appear as the dealership's TV spokesperson. But the catch was that the celebrity would only be in town that day, which was the day I got the call! Looking back, I did something I never did, which should have been an indication of the way the day would go. I took the call while I was in a planning meeting with another client, something I considered a no-no. But my friend sounded so desperate, I explained the situation to the other client and he was very gracious about letting me reschedule our meeting for the next day so I could help my dealer friend out of a major jam. I immediately called my cameraman, instructing him to drop whatever he was doing, and get over to the dealership as quickly as possible with a camera crew, telling him I'd meet him there within the hour. Have you ever agreed to do something, and then wondered to yourself, "Why am I doing this?"

Well, that's what I was asking myself. I work pretty fast, though, and in the car on the way over I conceived a couple of really good scripts that I thought would fit the personality of the celebrity. At this point, I should probably tell you that the celebrity was Foster Brooks, who made quite a name for himself on TV as *The Lovable Lush*. If you don't remember Foster, or perhaps he was way before your time, Foster earned his nickname as a lovable character with the habit of getting just a little tipsy, as evidenced by his (faked) slurred speech patterns. With white hair and white beard, he was a standout guy in any crowd. As I made my way to the dealership, it suddenly dawned on me that I had never worked with a Hollywood celebrity, let alone direct one, and I don't mind telling you that my nerves were getting the better of me!

You guessed it…ten minutes from the dealership I got involved in a fender bender. It was pretty minor, but my eyeglasses managed to get broken when my face hit the steering wheel on impact. My car wasn't in any condition to drive, so after enduring the police report-taking process, I called a cab to get me to the dealership, confident that even though I would be late, my cameraman would already be on site preparing to shoot the commercials I had half-prepared in transit. I arrived to find my dealer friend pacing his lot. I must have been quite a sight with a bump on the head and wearing the only glasses I could find, super dark prescription shades. "Where's my camera crew," I asked. "Your guy just called…he couldn't round up a crew, so he's on his way over by himself." I thought to myself, this is not a good sign. "Where's Mr. Brooks," I asked. "He's waiting in my office. He says he's got to be out of here in an hour, two tops!" This also was not a good sign. In the meantime, my cameraman had driven up, and he began unloading all the gear he would need for the shoot. I could see he was very nervous. So was I, to be perfectly honest! I limped into the dealer's office to find Foster sitting patiently on the couch, reading a magazine. I introduced myself, and he politely shook my hand with a look on his face that said *this isn't Hollywood, son, you can take off those ridiculous shades.* I explained about the accident on the way over, the loss of my glasses, rendering me virtually blind without them, and asked he would like to take a look at the scripts I had prepared. What I forgot to tell him was that I hadn't even had time to write them down yet! We spent the next fifteen minutes brainstorming cute little lines that would fit his character's personality. OK, they were corny, but *corny* equals *good* in Advertising. For example, "I just flew in from Vegas…(add the voice slur) *and boy-b-b-boy, are my ah-a-arms tired!*" We came up with a bunch more, and I started feeling a little better about the day. Until my cameraman came running into the office, red as a beet, screaming that the camera lens had just popped and he had to go find another one. To make a very long story as short as possible, we didn't get started shooting for another hour. We had no cue cards, no story boards, and no plan of action other than our one-liners scribbled on the back of a few available napkins! What struck me was that Foster never stopped smiling, no matter what happened. I really think he was getting a kick out of all this!

Once we finally got shooting, everything went pretty smoothly, despite the 90-degree mid-summer heat of the day. When we were finished, we had shot enough footage for a total of seven TV spots, which magically turned into ten when I used the most hilarious out-takes to create three additional spots that no one could have predicted. Foster was not only a gem to work with, he was a true gentleman. Not once did he stop smiling, not once did he complain about anything. He made my job so easy it was embarrassing. All I had to do was give him the countdown…5…4…3…2…1…action…and he did the rest, script or no script. Believe me when I tell you, he had a built-in mental alarm clock that pinched him at the 29-second point of each take! Hours after his original "must leave" deadline, we wrapped it up, and Foster was on his way back to the airport to catch the next flight back to wherever he had flown in from. What a pro!

No more than a week after the TV campaign hit the air, my dealer friend called me, asking if I could come over. It seems he had just received a letter from a local group, complaining that his dealership was promoting drinking and driving by using Foster as spokesperson in their commercials. My friend was totally ticked, to put it mildly, and he wanted to call them and give them a piece of his mind. I convinced him not to do that. Instead, I took the letter and crafted my own response as the creator of the commercials. In a nutshell, my letter was extremely polite and sensitively written. After all, I shared their goal of discouraging drinking while driving. I tried to make the distinction between a sense of humor in a TV spot, and the task of educating our young people about the dangers of drinking and driving. To be sure, the commercials *never* made any reference to driving *or* drinking. I concluded my letter by asking the group members if they were aware that this same car dealer had just donated a $20,000 automobile to a local charity to use as a raffled fund-raiser. A week later, I received a delightful return letter from the group, apologizing for "jumping the gun" in their first letter of complaint. As a result, rather than antagonize an influential local citizens group, we were successful in establishing a friendly relationship that eventually resulted in a hefty financial donation from the dealer.

The second incident was nowhere near the fiasco I just described, but it relates a story you just won't believe! I had produced a TV spot for a carpet store to run on the Labor Day weekend, announcing a special one-day holiday sale. Picture this TV commercial, if you dare. It opened with a group of 25 *very* pregnant women peering in the door of the store, waiting for the doors to open for the sale. The young salesman (an actor) looks out at them in bewilderment, and opens the doors, only to be virtually trampled by the stampeding moms-to-be. Now flat on his back, he can't figure out what's going on, but then it suddenly hits him as the audio portion of the commercial explains the nature of the sale..."Free *Delivery*...No Extra Charge for *Labor*..." you get the idea, right? OK, OK, I'm sorry. But it really was funny, at least to me, being an ignorant male, and young to boot! In truth, my wife had warned me about this one, but as usual, I didn't listen. Big mistake, but what else is new? It was Labor Day, I had the day off, and I was enjoying a leisurely breakfast at home with my wife, when the phone rang. I answered it, and was greeted by a rather irate sounding woman. "Young man, I know I'm bothering you at your home, and I'm sorry for that, but you certainly deserve anything you get with that terribly insulting commercial you made for that carpet store. You should be ashamed of yourself!" You know, she was right. I was ashamed! And I told her so, asking her to have mercy on a creatively overworked ad guy. The more I groveled, the more I had a strange feeling I just couldn't seem to shake. Then it hit me! "Excuse me, but how did you know my name and my home phone number?" She answered, "I asked the store manager, and he was kind enough to give me your name and home phone number." Something still didn't click in my mind, and I began to notice the commotion in the background from her side of the call, so I asked her, "Umm, where are you calling me from?" She paused (earlier in another chapter I used the phrase "pregnant pause," but I won't do that to you here!) and eventually replied, "Oh…well…I'm over at the carpet store, if you really must know." She had me now. "What are you doing there, if I might ask?" Her answer floored me, you should excuse another pun. "Well…I came in here to complain to the store manager about your insulting commercial, and they were so nice to me, and I needed new carpet, so I bought a house full while I was here, since it was on sale. But I wanted you to know I didn't approve of your commercial!"

Yes, it really happened. Honest! Lessons, lessons, lessons. The one to be learned here is that no matter how hard you try, someone, somewhere will be offended by something you say or do in your Advertising. Don't fight it. Roll with it. You'll be much happier that **You've Got A Friend.** (Thank you, Carole King!)

THE END

I hope you've enjoyed meeting some of the *People* I've introduced you to along my journey. And I hope I've been at least partially successful in helping you gain a new insight to some **Secrets** of Advertising. Remember, this isn't brain surgery, after all! If I've done a good job in this writing, you'll come away with the realization that the essence of your own Advertising is undoubtedly locked away within your own thoughts and ideas, awaiting magical release through a process that can only be described as cosmically pre-ordained. You may find that release all by yourself, or you may be lucky enough to find it with **A Little Help From My Friends.** (Thank you, Ringo!) I've merely tried to give you the key to unlock some of the mysteries.

The end of a book is just that. A common misconception is that Advertising is the end. If you think that, you will have missed the point of this book, as well as the point of Advertising, which is no more than a means to an end, that end being whatever you define it to be in your realm of goals. If you revisit the **Introduction,** you'll be reminded that this book was all about throwing a successful party at your place of business, every day. Advertising is the means you employ to make sure everyone knows about your party and decides to attend, convinced they'll enjoy a good time. The difference between your business party and your house party is that the latter is perhaps a once-a-year special event, whereas the former is a daily affair. As exhausted as you may feel after all the preparation and expense of throwing your business party, you've got to do it again, and again, and again. And make no mistake. Some parties will be better than others. Even Babe Ruth didn't hit a home run every time at the plate. If I'm not mistaken, he was also the strikeout king! But he didn't stop swinging the bat, did he? This is my way of telling you that Advertising must be an ongoing, consistent effort. As with everything, the more you do it, the better it gets. Look at it another way. What happens when you stop?

The end.

ABOUT THE AUTHOR

Jeff Resnick is a man of varied talents, skills and abilities. His "chosen profession" was as a college Professor of Music in the State University of New York, where he was honored as a 1977 recipient of the prestigious *New York State Chancellor's Award for Excellence in Teaching*. He's a published composer, arranger, recording studio musician and producer, with several albums to his credit. Jeff's musical arrangements have been performed by internationally acclaimed Jazz artists, and his commercial music productions are licensed nationwide for TV, radio and film. He left academia in 1978 and founded an advertising, marketing and production agency, which he nurtured into a nationally syndicated company. His specialty was increasing market share for thousands of retail businesses throughout the United States and Canada, often under the auspices of national franchise companies, cooperative buying groups, manufacturers and trade associations. He has conceptualized, planned, developed, produced, implemented and managed all variety of local, regional and national advertising and marketing programs in virtually every media market in the US. An accomplished public speaker, he has designed and delivered educational advertising seminars and workshops to thousands of business owners and managers at their national conventions, trade shows and buying markets. (More than a few TV, radio and newspaper executives were known to sneak in uninvited!) His award-winning advertising campaigns have been displayed at trade shows in several industries, and syndicated to over 1,000 businesses. After concluding the sale of his agency, Jeff embarked on his search for Truth and Beauty, only to discover the inescapable inner need to cleanse his soul by writing about some of the people he met and worked with during his 20-year advertising trek. A native of Rochester, NY, he and Cass, his wife of 32 years, currently live in Williamsburg, VA, only a short walk from the famous historic district. Jeff remains an active advertising and marketing consultant, always open to consideration of interesting and challenging new projects. He's also an accomplished musician, specializing in the performance of classic Jazz and Pop standards in a contemporary musical environment. And, he is Visiting Professor of Advertising and Marketing at West Virginia University for the 2001-2 academic year. If you'd like more information about Jeff's musical performances and school workshops, or his retail advertising campaigns still in syndication, you may visit him on the Internet at www.jeffresnick.com.